Praise for *Sex in the Snow*

"*Sex in the Snow* is a serious and intriguing analysis of a nation and society in transition."

— *Maclean's*

"Recommended reading — Hot on the heels of David Foot's much-discussed *Boom, Bust and Echo* comes *Sex in the Snow* ... the book wastes little time in telling us Foot's school of demographics fails to paint a complete picture."

— *Marketing* magazine

"Breezy and saucy... Adams argues that many business and government institutions are in a state of denial about Canadians' newfound feistiness ... [His] central point, that we are not prisoners of our demography, will resonate for all politicians struggling with ideas about distinct society and Canadian nationalism ... He also has valuable insights for business: that Canadians are relying less on employers and government to take care for them; that new corporate entities and networks will emerge as Canadians express their individuality; and that Canada will draw closer to the United States economically, while remaining culturally distinct."

— *Report on Business* magazine

"The premise of massive cultural change throws down a challenge to the demographic prognosticators ... The notion of tribes fragments easy demographic generalizations based on age and gender. Adams's challenge goes further than that, however. His argument that a revolution in values has occurred means that traditional assessments based on the life-cycle, previous behaviour by gender, class or ethnicity, have all become suspect ... Adams's book has much to offer. It is a useful corrective to the determinism of popular demography."

— *The Globe and Mail*

"[Adams's] provocative statements are worth considering ... the fun in reading *Sex in the Snow* is in trying to decide which tribe is yours ... we see ourselves in a mirror — and the reflection prompts us to think about who is behind the face staring back."

— *The Daily News* (Halifax)

"[*Sex in the Snow*] portrays citizens' diversity. Based on in-depth surveys of our social values and scientific investigations of the underlying motivations that propel our culture, it reveals the evolution of the Canadian character, and forecasts our future directions."

— *Northern Daily News*

"An overview of changing Canadian society ... a new original look into the souls of Canadians ... *Sex in the Snow* is an important guidebook for a country in a time of transition ... Adams's work gives a new and sometimes startling picture of Canadians ... *Sex in the Snow* is engagingly written."

—*The Leader-Post* (Regina)

"[Adams] is on target when he discusses the diminishment of established authority and the rise of the priority of choice in all spheres of life. He also helps us understand what might be behind Ontario's sudden swing to the political right."

— *The Record* (Kitchener-Waterloo)

"Illuminating and worth pondering ... an earnest, intriguing and occasionally glib description of the social attitudes of Canadians ... the categories are a handy form of explanation ... armed with them, you might have some fun analyzing the next federal election or the odd panic that grips people — even snowbound Canadians — at the mere mention of a millennium."

— *The Expositor* (Brantford)

"Bottom line? *Sex in the Snow* is both thought-provoking and fun."

— *Calgary Herald*

PENGUIN CANADA

SEX IN THE SNOW

MICHAEL ADAMS is president of the Environics group of marketing research and communications consulting companies with offices in the United States and Canada. He has written three bestselling books, including *Fire and Ice: The United States, Canada, and the Myth of Converging Values*, which won the prestigious 2004 Donner Prize for the best book on public policy in Canada.

Also by Michael Adams

Better Happy Than Rich?
Canadians, Money and the Meaning of Life

Fire and Ice
The United States, Canada, and the Myth of Converging Values

American Backlash
The Untold Story of Social Change in the United States

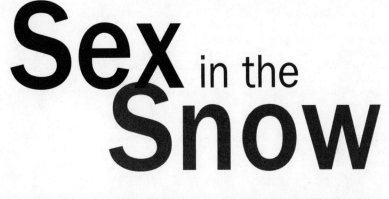

Sex in the Snow

THE SURPRISING REVOLUTION
IN CANADIAN SOCIAL VALUES

MICHAEL ADAMS

PENGUIN
CANADA

PENGUIN CANADA

Published by the Penguin Group

Penguin Group (Canada), 90 Eglinton Avenue East, Suite 700, Toronto, Ontario, Canada M4P 2Y3
    (a division of Pearson Canada Inc.)

Penguin Group (USA) Inc., 375 Hudson Street, New York, New York 10014, U.S.A.
Penguin Books Ltd, 80 Strand, London WC2R 0RL, England
Penguin Ireland, 25 St Stephen's Green, Dublin 2, Ireland (a division of Penguin Books Ltd)
Penguin Group (Australia), 250 Camberwell Road, Camberwell, Victoria 3124, Australia
    (a division of Pearson Australia Group Pty Ltd)
Penguin Books India Pvt Ltd, 11 Community Centre, Panchsheel Park, New Delhi – 110 017, India
Penguin Group (NZ), cnr Airborne and Rosedale Roads, Albany, Auckland 1310, New Zealand
    (a division of Pearson New Zealand Ltd)
Penguin Books (South Africa) (Pty) Ltd, 24 Sturdee Avenue, Rosebank, Johannesburg 2196, South Africa

Penguin Books Ltd, Registered Offices: 80 Strand, London WC2R 0RL, England

First published in a Viking Canada hardcover by Penguin Group (Canada), a division of Pearson Canada Inc., 1997
Published in Penguin Canada paperback by Penguin Group (Canada), a division of Pearson Canada Inc., 1998
Published in this edition, 2006

(WEB) 10 9 8 7 6 5 4 3 2 1

Manufactured in Canada.

LIBRARY AND ARCHIVES CANADA CATALOGUING IN PUBLICATION

Adams, Michael, 1946 Sept. 29–
    Sex in the snow : the surprising revolution in Canadian social values / Michael Adams.

ISBN-13: 978-0-14-305234-0
ISBN-10: 0-14-305234-9 : $22.00

1. Canada—Social conditions—1991– . 2. Social values—Canada. 3. National characteristics, Canadian.
4. Social prediction—Canada. 5. Canada—Population. I. Title.

HB3529.A33 2006   306.0971009'0511   C2006-903552-0

Visit the Penguin Group (Canada) website at **www.penguin.ca**

Special and corporate bulk purchase rates available; please see
www.penguin.ca/corporatesales or call 1-800-399-6858, ext. 477 or 474

For my friends

Acknowledgments

I have written this book in honour of Yvan Corbeil, the founder and president of CROP from 1965 to 1990, and Alain de Vulpian, who founded Cofremca in 1954. These men, one from Quebec, the other from France, have been the two great mentors of my professional life. I have also written this book for my children, Marion and William, and for my life partner and much respected fellow researcher, Donna Dasko, so they will know their father, and their spouse, in another way, through the medium of the printed word.

I owe a great debt to my business partners Alain Giguère, president of CROP Inc. of Montreal, Larry Kaagan, president of Kaagan Research Associates in New York City, and Mike Heffring, president of Environics West in Calgary. Alain, who succeeded Yvan Corbeil at CROP, has done more than any other individual to adapt Alain de Vulpian's system of tracking social change (3SC) to a North American context. Larry, who assisted Daniel Yankelovich with his seminal book *New Rules*, published in 1981, established the 3SC system in the United States in 1992. And it was Mike who first suggested the idea of an analysis of generational values that is the core of this book.

sex in the snow

Like all survey research, the book itself is a collaborative effort, with three of my colleagues forming a team for this project. Stephen Popiel performed the multivariate statistical magic or, as some would joke, "tortured the data till they told the truth." Sean Saraq and Mary Jane Lennon debated, drafted and edited my ideas and hypotheses over the many months it took to write this book. In many ways, they represented the yin and yang that are present in the title of the book — the spontaneity and hedonism of post-modern Canada, within the context of the enduring values that have always set us apart as Canadians. The entire team owes its gratitude to Barry Watson, Environics' executive vice-president, and our company chairman, Derek Ruston, both of whom supported us throughout the project.

Thank you to Jennifer Maddock for providing the graphics. And finally, I would like to thank my agent, Bruce Westwood, and my publisher, Cynthia Good, two of the best impresarios in the world of ideas. They believed I could be persuasive in print as well as over a glass of Chardonnay; I hope you agree.

Table of Contents

Preface

When *Sex in the Snow* was first published a decade ago, it was released into a country newly in love with the wonders of demography. The insightful University of Toronto economist David Foot had just written a book that would become a monumental bestseller. *Boom, Bust and Echo* helped Canadians make sense of many of the changes they saw around them. It showed them how people's ages and life stages could inform all kinds of personal attitudes and behaviours, which could in turn, on a mass scale, drive enormous social trends.

Just as marketers, policymakers and the informed public were becoming attuned to the tremendous power of demographic forces, *Sex in the Snow* came along to complicate things. In this book I argued that demography is not always destiny. I claimed that values can be even more important than demographic traits when it comes to informing people's behaviour as citizens, consumers, employees, parents, friends and spiritual beings. Demography could explain some things, but not everything: some old men aren't grumpy; some girls don't just want to have fun.

Exploring differences among Canadians in different chronological stages of their lives was one of the key projects of the book. We divided our three generations — Elder, Boomer and Generation X — into a total of twelve "tribes" according to the social values they expressed in our annual surveys. In many cases, values transcended demographics. For example, the Cosmopolitan Modernists — an Elder tribe with flexible, postmodern values and a thirst for experience — resembled some of our youth tribes much more closely than they resembled their own more traditional age peers.

Another important project of *Sex in the Snow* was to refute the old saw that the more things change the more they stay the same. In our data we found evidence that important intergenerational values changes were afoot in Canada, and that these changes could not be attributed merely to life-stage factors. Certainly, there were young rebels in our sample (some with causes and some without), but there was more than youthful rebellion going on here. Canadians, once a shy, deferential, self-denying people, were becoming more confident, more focused on immediate gratification and soft hedonism, and above all more committed to personal autonomy. This profound values shift began with some trendsetting Elders born before 1945, gained force with the idealistic Baby Boomers born between 1946 and 1966, and became the assumed norm among the Gen Xers born in 1967 and later.

What changes have transpired between the original publication of *Sex in the Snow* and the release of this edition a decade on? Remarkably, more of the same: Canadians continue to embrace ever more postmodern values.

The first social institution any of us is ever exposed to is the family. A decade ago, I described Canadians' growing flexibility when it came to matters of home and family. Increasingly, Canadians believed that Father didn't *necessarily* know best; he still might in some cases but he wasn't the boss by default. Family leadership could be flexible. Similarly, gender roles were becoming more malleable: growing proportions of Canadians believed not only that Mom could gain an equal footing with Dad in the professional sphere, but that domestic concerns — home and kids — were just as much men's responsibility as women's. And finally, although the issue of same-sex marriage was still years away from being on the public policy agenda in 1997, we found that Canadians were increasingly open to same-sex relationships, common-law partnerships and other non-traditional family arrangements.

These views have held steady, and in some cases grown. Upon *Sex in the Snow*'s release in 1997, the proportion of Canadians agreeing with the statement that "The father of the family must be master in his own house" was 19 per cent. In 2005, it was about the same: 18 per cent. In 1997 the proportion of Canadians agreeing that "Men have a certain natural superiority over women and nothing can change this" was 23 per cent. In 2005 it was 22 per cent.

On matters of family organization, values have continued to move toward flexibility and diversity. In 1997, 48 per cent of Canadians agreed that "Getting married and having children is the only real def-inition of a family." By 2005, agreement had declined to 38 per cent. Over the same period, support for the idea that "Society should regard people of the same sex who live together as being the same as a married couple" climbed from 39 per cent to 56 per cent. Common-law unions, once known as "living in sin," are now more likely to be known as "marriages not forged in a fiery crucible of seating plans, caterers and extended family." They are a virtual non-issue. In 1996, nearly seven in ten Canadians (68 per cent) agreed that "Society should regard people who live together without being married as being a family." By 2005, the proportion viewing common-law unions and marriages as equivalent was up to three-quarters (76 per cent).

In short, Canadians' attitudes about gender and family, once informed by rigid religious codes, are now much more heavily driven by values of autonomy and fulfillment — the belief that people should be able to choose the family arrangements that work best for them in both practical and emotional terms.

Flexibility and openness to diversity have also persisted in matters ethno-cultural. In 2002, the Pew Global Attitudes survey centre found that Canadians are by far the most likely of any Western society to believe that immigrants have a positive influence on their country. Fully three-quarters of Canadians (77 per cent), as compared to half of Americans (49 per cent) and smaller proportions throughout Western Europe, believe that the overall influence of immigrants is positive.

Given this exceptionally positive attitude toward newcomers to Canada, it is not surprising that our values surveys continue to find enthusiasm for the coexistence of people of diverse backgrounds and a cultural fusion that seeks to savour and explore — not elimi-nate — differences across races and heritages. Since 2000, the proportion of Canadians agreeing that "Other cultures have a lot to teach us; contact with them is enriching for us" has remained steady at 75 per cent. The proportion agreeing that "I would like to introduce my children to as many different cultures as possible—Western cultures as well as those from other parts of the world (Africa, etc.)" has climbed from 75 per cent to 83 per cent.

As I look back over the past decade, I marvel at how we continue to evolve along the trajectory our data charted in 1997. The continuation of that pattern would be less remarkable if our demographics were not changing so rapidly. Every year, Canada accepts around 200,000 new immigrants. Since the publication of *Sex in the Snow*, then, Canada has gained over 1.5 million people from all over the globe, most of whom settle in one of our three big cities. One in five Canadians is now foreign-born. If we include in that number those whose parents were born outside Canada, it climbs to two in five.

Along with their belongings and their hopes for a bright future in their new country, these new Canadians bring with them values from every corner of the planet. Many of the societies from which they hail embrace deeply traditional values; they are more religious, more deferential to authority and have more traditional ideas about gender and racial mixing than is common among those born in Canada.

A question much discussed these days — and likely for years to come, as Canada's low birth rates make the apparent need for immigrants ever greater — is the extent to which the children of these new Canadians absorb the values of their adoptive country. When we hear of young people born in Canada embracing fundamentalisms spawned elsewhere in the world, or when we learn of newcomers to Canada clinging bitterly to the social divisions and hostilities of their homelands, some inevitably ask whether multiculturalism as we know it is a big mistake.

Some children of new Canadians, like some children of Canadian-born parents, will have trouble navigating a society full of fluid and overlapping identities. For most, though, diversity and flexibility are simply a given — and sometimes an exciting and liberating one. Young people in Canada, particularly in Canadian cities, go to multicultural schools, live in multicultural communities and encounter a multiplicity of languages and races every time they get on a bus, go shopping or visit a library. Almost all develop associations with peers of diverse backgrounds, many develop close friendships, and some will even go on to marry and raise children with a partner who might have been unimaginable to their grandparents.

Values data indicate that children of new Canadians are as comfortable as anyone in a diverse Canada. When we look at the values of Canadians aged fifteen to twenty-nine who are the children of two foreign-born parents, we find tremendous openness to people of other backgrounds. Eight in ten (79 per cent) agree that "Other cultures have a lot to teach us; contact with them is enriching for us." Seventy-two per cent of those with Canadian-born parents agree. Eighty-three per cent of young people with foreign-born parents agree that "I would like to introduce my children to as many different cultures as possible — Western cultures as well as those from other parts of the world (Africa, etc.)." Three-quarters (76 per cent) of those with Canadian-born parents say the same.

People are individuals; some will always be attracted to rigid ideologies, and a smaller number will be attracted to violence. But there is much evidence — not just polling data, but the evidence many of us see in our daily lives — to suggest that Canadian multiculturalism is working. I find it truly remarkable that despite the huge number of immigrants Canada accepts each year — and the sheer diversity of values, attitudes and cultural frameworks that coexist in our society — somehow Canadians new and old continue to travel a trajectory of basic egalitarianism and harmony.

If I had to sum it up in a few words, I would say that Canada is becoming more Canadian. Evolving away from its old colonial mentality (whether a colony of France, of Great Britain or of the United States), Canada is becoming ever more itself. If this sounds to you like an ambiguous projection of where we are headed, you are reading it correctly. No one knows for sure where this great experiment in humanity will lead. I have my data, my hypotheses and, yes, my hopes for where we are going. And when I walk the streets of Vancouver, Toronto and Montreal and see people from all over the world — especially young people — not just tolerating but savouring one another, I can't help but feel we are on the right track, albeit a track that would have been inconceivable to the fathers of confederation. There is no question that abundant challenges accompany the ongoing invention of this country. But I believe that the values ordinary Canadians express in our surveys are perhaps the best tools any society can have for living well, and long, on a small planet.

Michael Adams
August 2006

Introduction

I have been a pollster in Canada for twenty-five years. Together with my associates at Environics, I have conducted hundreds of focus groups and thousands of surveys among several million Canadians and, more recently, among many thousands of Americans, as my company extends its scope into the United States. Like Blanche Dubois in Tennessee Williams's *Streetcar Named Desire,* we pollsters depend upon the "kindness of strangers." We phone them at home and knock on their doors, often at inconvenient times. Yet, miraculously, people generally cooperate, and mostly without compensation. We add up their answers, calculate weights and percentages and report the results to our clients, who pay us handsomely for the information. It is a remarkable business when you think about it, not least because of the opportunity it affords to keep one's finger on the pulse of public sentiment from month to month, year to year, and decade to decade. When Curious George grows up, he'll become a pollster.

The turbulent decade of the 1960s has been described as a watershed in the history of the Western world. It was the decade in which, seemingly en masse, people began to question many, if not all, of the basic assumptions that shaped the way they viewed themselves and the world around them. This mass re-evaluation of life's basic rule-book set in motion a sometimes unsettling, and always exciting, revolution in social values. And it is the legacy of that upheaval that I am writing about in *Sex in the Snow*.

My purpose in writing this book is to describe for my fellow Canadians the psychological landscape of their country in a way that will help them better understand Canadians in general, their friends and their co-workers, and — if I'm not being too presumptuous — their parents, their children, their spouses and significant others, and maybe even themselves. Like George Gallup, who helped found our profession earlier this century and who co-authored with Canadian Saul Rae the important book *The Pulse of Democracy* in 1940[1], I believe polling advances the cause of democratic civilization. Know better your neighbours and you will better know yourself. A more accurate knowledge of self and society will, in my view, go a long way to improve the quality of our lives and our relations with others.

In the unofficial version of the King James Bible, it is reported that Adam once said to Eve: "We live in a time of transition." You may have heard this cliché before, if not this particular joke. The fact is, there has been change or transition in every era of human history. What distinguishes the last quarter century is the pace and scope of change. Identify a "cutting edge" trend and, within months, it can be mainstream, or even passé.

Since my first days as a pollster, the rate of change has

been accelerating to the point where, by the mid-1980s, my colleagues and I began witnessing some unexpected and seemingly arbitrary shifts in public opinion. It became clear to me that part of the equation of public attitudes *vis-à-vis* political and consumer issues was missing. The much-vaunted volatility in opinion polls was, in reality, a reflection of much deeper changes in the values of our culture. The world-views and belief systems of Canadians were changing.

In the early 1980s, I started attending international conferences of market researchers and pollsters. At one such conference in New Jersey, I met fellow Canadian Yvan Corbeil (where else do Canadians meet?), the president of the Montreal-based polling firm CROP. Yvan and I became instant friends when we discovered our mutual interest in the dynamics of social change. He had been polling Canadians since 1965, when he founded CROP (le Centre de Recherche sur l'Opinion Publique). In that sense, we were contemporaries, as it was just five years later that I had co-founded Environics in Toronto. Like me, Yvan had become convinced that the volatility we were witnessing in public opinion and consumer behaviour reflected deeper changes in the values of Canadians, and that Canadian values needed to be understood in the context of our Euro-American roots. "We are re-inventing what it means to be human," he said to me, "and it is our duty to help our clients pilot this change for their organizations." He told me, as we walked together through the woods around the conference centre, how his quest for understanding social change had led him to visit Paris in the 1970s. It was here that he came across the pioneering work of Alain de Vulpian, the president of the firm Cofremca.

I will never forget that day, as Yvan talked to me about hedonism, sensualism, pursuit of intensity and emotional experiences, flexibility of personality, and other trends identified and tracked by the Cofremca system. For a political scientist who had spent his life trying to figure out how people might vote in the next election, or how strongly ("very" or "somewhat") they felt about foreign investment or capital punishment, this was pretty heady stuff. I knew this knowledge would help me understand the growing volatility in the behaviour of consumers and voters. I knew "values" would be important for the future of Environics.

Cofremca began tracking social change in France in the early 1970s, and, by the late 1970s, had exported its unique system to other Western European countries. This research is now conducted in each of the G7 countries, with the exception of Japan. The first survey on this continent was undertaken by CROP in 1983. Soon thereafter, Environics and CROP began working together, first on tracking public opinion for *The Globe and Mail* beginning in 1984, and later on tracking social change. In 1989, in partnership with CROP, Environics brought the Cofremca research system — the 3SC Social Values Monitor — to English Canada. Then, in 1992, in association with our American affiliate, Kaagan Research Associates, we took the system to the United States.

The 3SC Social Values Monitor tracks trends in the underlying social values of Canadians, Americans and Europeans.
"3SC" stands for *Système Cofremca de Suivi des Courants
Socio-Culturels* — the Cofremca System for Tracking Socio-
cultural Trends. In French, three Ss and three Cs. The
information collected for the 3SC Monitor has important
implications, not just for governments and for businesses,
but for anyone interested in where we, as a society, now
stand, and how we got where we are. Along the journey of
self-discovery, some of which is described in this book, I
hope to dispel some myths about Canada's national character, and perhaps suggest where Canadians and other post-
modern people around the world may be heading in upcom-
ing decades.

A few years ago my parents, William and Florentine, asked
me what I had learned about Canadians after all these
years of polling. Typical of my own brand of irony, I
responded by telling them Woody Allen's joke: "I once took
a speed-reading course and they gave me Tolstoy's *War
and Peace* ... it's about Russia." Anyway, you two, here is
a somewhat more detailed answer to your question. And if
you wonder why it took me twenty-five years to put it down
on paper, remember that this is the country that cele-
brates and lives diversity, like no other place on earth.
Making generalizations that hit the mark about such a population is tough enough, and even tougher when the target
is a moving one. As the pre-Socratic philosopher Heraclitus
noted, there is no being, only becoming.

sex in the snow

I have learned that Canadians, like people everywhere, have changed in ways that reflect American and global influences. But, these changes are expressed in a uniquely Canadian manner. When an American wins the lottery, he buys a Cadillac to show off to his friends. The lucky Canadian uses her winnings to buy an airline ticket to someplace else. American hedonism is more material; ours is more experiential.

As I see it, the new mental posture of Canadians has been shaped by three major quests: for personal autonomy, for pleasure and for spiritual fulfilment. In all three pursuits, the accent is on "personal." It is this particular constellation of socio-cultural currents — among the most profound in Canada today — that gave rise to the title *Sex in the Snow.* The snow represents what is most enduring in Canadian values; the sex represents the hedonism and demand for immediate gratification that distinguishes the recent evolution of social values in the country. The stereotype of Canadians as respectful and reserved, and not that imaginative, is fast losing its validity.

During the past quarter century, Canada has been transformed by a social revolution, not the Marxist variety my classmates hoped for in the late 1960s, but a peaceful revolution in the structure of authority in our society. It is the shift from an authoritarian pyramid to a "heterarchical" model of how society should function, and how people should interact. Not a *hier*archical model, but not *an*archical either. Pragmatic, flexible, and egalitarian.

This social revolution represents a radical transformation in the psyche of average Canadians that enables them to define and redefine themselves in ways that, in the past, were the prerogative of only a tiny, wealthy élite. In this revolution, the societally defined and often self-imposed stereotypes and roles prescribed for each of us have been questioned, modified and often discarded. We now invent and reinvent ourselves.

This revolution in social values is, in my view, as profound as the liberal-democratic revolutions of the eighteenth and nineteenth centuries. Then, white, property-owning males seized power from feudal lords, dukes and bishops. The élite, under the banner of universal rights and equality for all, expanded from 1 per cent to 10 per cent of the population. The social revolution we are now witnessing realizes the values of that earlier revolution by extending the franchise of choice from 10 per cent to close to 100 per cent — in essence, to all of us. Though the ideas of freedom and equality are not new, their actualization on such a grand scale is. And in many ways, Canada and its citizens are leading the way into this new world. The status associated with once-cherished institutions, both feudal and those created by liberal democracy — churches, legislative bodies and professional élites (politicians, lawyers, doctors and the clergy) — has gone into steep decline. Established authority has had its legitimacy questioned in every sphere.

The day after the Charlottetown accord was defeated, the CBC's "Morningside" host, Peter Gzowski, invited then minister of justice Kim Campbell and me to render our impressions. When asked what lesson she had learned from the referendum defeat, Ms. Campbell said, "We have to come up with a better way to educate the Canadian people." "No," I instantly retorted, "the Canadian people are going to have to come up with a better way to educate their politicians."

Many have been slow to learn the lesson, to see the new social revolution and act accordingly. This is particularly true for the public and private monopolies and oligopolies that have traditionally run the show in Canada. A case in point was the debacle in January 1995 over the introduction of eight new specialty channels for Canadian cable viewers. Some cable companies, including the country's largest, Rogers Cablesystems, presented the new channels in such a way that failure to subscribe to them would result in the loss of some popular, established channels. In addition, the cable companies used the system of "negative option" billing, whereby the customer was automatically charged for the new services, unless he or she specifically opted out. Although the additional charge for the new channels was minimal — two to four dollars per month — the public was outraged. Rogers was accused of "mugging" its customers, and federal and provincial legislators were deluged with angry calls; fax machines were jammed and one MP reported that his answering machine had broken down under the pressure. Within four days of bringing the new channels on line, Rogers called a news conference that addressed both of these concerns. Company executives made a rare public admission that they had "made a mistake" and that their marketing techniques "had acquired connotations of corporate arrogance and duplicity." Admittedly, this "tempest in a teapot" did not have the political impact, for instance, of the rejection of the Charlottetown accord. But, it was a sort of wake-up call for many of those surprised at the ferocity of the consumer revolt. What the incident proved, beyond doubt, was that the deference and loyalty of Canadians could no longer be taken for granted, even if many of their business and government leaders were still in a radical state of denial.

Over the past three decades, the Canadian personality has evolved from one that could be described as shy and mostly deferential to one that is characterized by a more autonomous and ironic individualism. Well-documented "demographic" changes have been complemented, and sometimes eclipsed, by even more significant "psychographic" changes. Relative affluence, access to education, travel and information has resulted in growing numbers of Canadians being able to transcend the traditional demographic categories of age, gender, religion, social class and ethnicity, and to then define themselves in novel ways. As I see it, this new flexibility, when combined with advanced communications technology, opens up almost limitless possibilities for personal definition and redefinition in the century ahead.

The word "demography" is from the Greek word *demos*, meaning "the people." When sociologists write about "the people," they often divide personal demographic character-istics into two categories. The first is defined as "ascribed" characteristics; it includes all those personal identifiers over which — *pace* Michael Jackson — people have no control, such as age, ethnicity, race and sex. The second category is defined as "achieved" characteristics; it includes those identifiers over which we have at least some control, such as income, occupation and education.

It is the thesis of this book that the old saw "demography is destiny" is no longer true, at least for Canadians, and par-ticularly for young Canadians. Demographic characteristics *influence* people's social values, but they do not *determine* them to the extent they once did. Demography may not yet be dead, but it is certainly less reliable as a predictor of values than at any time in the past.

The "demography is destiny" school of thought sees the story of the human journey as a series of passages through more or less inevitable life-cycle stages: birth, childhood, adolescence, marriage, family, retirement, death. Economists and investment bankers operate on the propo-sition that there are ultimately only two important human motives that guide people's behaviour through this journey: fear and greed. Of course, there is some truth in this per-spective, but it is not the whole truth, nor even close to it. Further, whatever truth there may have been in this assumption is diminishing as we become a more complex and malleable culture. Our research has identified about eighty motivators, not just two. We see an incredible range of values configurations and life-cycle choices as humans defy the old laws and spirit of demographic gravity.

Some prominent Canadian economists have recently argued that changes in the demographic composition of our society are precipitating a return to "family values," and that the aging of the baby-boom generation will inevitably mean a dramatic increase in the savings rate of Canadians. However, our analysis of Canadian social values predicts no such return to either social or economic traditionalism. If the aging of the baby boomers were to produce an increase in the savings rate of Canadians, this increase would be apparent, since a lot of boomers have already hit the forty-year mark. Instead, we have seen a decline in the savings rate, from 10.2 per cent in 1992, to 9.5 per cent in 1993, to 7.9 per cent in 1994, to 7.4 per cent in 1995. Likewise, the personal-savings rate in the United States has fallen since the 1970s, whereas Japan and Germany continue to have high rates. These phenomena reflect deeper cultural forces, not some predetermined notion of what people inevitably do at various ages. If economists and demographers wish to better predict human behaviour, they might pay closer attention to the changing values and motivations of their fellow Canadians.

At the turn of the century, we Canadians had a life expectancy of about fifty years. Today, it is over seventy-five. A hundred years ago, life, for nearly everyone, *was* a series of almost inevitable life-cycle passages. To say then that fear, guilt and greed were the main motivations of human behaviour was closer to the mark, though still a crude approximation. Today the "inevitable" life-cycle stages — other than birth and death — are anything but inevitable, or even necessarily sequential. A man can father a child — and sometimes does — in all but one decade of his life, and medical advances have now expanded the fertility options of women. Just as the VCR allows us to time-shift our favourite programs, "the Pill" and our will allow us to procreate and re-create our lives in ways our ancestors could not have imagined. Why can't one's career precede child-rearing? Why can't education happen at intervals, like meals in a day: at the beginning, middle and near the end of one's life?

An aging population may, in fact, be embracing family values, but by no means are these the classic family values exemplified by the 1950s ideal of a (non-working) mom, a gainfully employed dad and 2.5 kids. In Canada today, the model for "family values" has evolved from "Leave It to Beaver" to "Murphy Brown." In my parents' generation, rebellion was marriage between a Catholic and a Protestant, or a Protestant and a Jew. For my generation, the baby boomers, rebellion was common-law marriage, or divorce for those who did marry. For Generation X, rebellion is interracial unions, or the normalization of gay and lesbian relationships.

Sure, there is nostalgia for a simpler set of ubiquitous and enduring values. What else accounts for the continuing popular interest in shows like "I Love Lucy," or the resurgence of Jane Austen's novels? But "simple" is not how we live our lives today, nor does this nostalgia reflect the values that motivate many of the important decisions Canadians make at work, at home or at the shopping centre.

But let us return to demography. Demographers often make categorical statements about the behaviour of generations. They assume, for example, that inexorable laws of life-stage rule our lives, as instinct orders a hive of bees. Intuitively, we know these simplifications are far from the truth. Experience confirms our intuition. Take, for example, a fifty-year-old man. If demography is destiny, then this man got married in his mid-twenties, fathered one or two children in the late 1960s or early 1970s, has launched these kids into the world, and is beginning to think about retirement and mortality. This may be true for some fifty-year-old guys. And it was undoubtedly more true in the 1950s, when values were more homogeneous and traditional, and there was a sense that "if you know one middle-class Canadian, you know them all." This stereotype was never *completely* true, but it is more untrue today than ever.

In an otherwise very positive *Globe and Mail* review of David Foot's recent bestseller *Boom, Bust and Echo* — a book I very much enjoyed — urban planner Joe Berridge makes what I consider to be a valid point: "Ultimately, demographics tells us nothing, of course. We draw our own conclusions from the data and hope that the future will be like the past. That it won't be entirely is also true, however hard

Foot squeezes the numbers — technology, feminism, mass media, globalization and other powerful drivers of contemporary society are largely independent of demographics or caught in a more tangled web of causation."[2]

Back in Walkerton, Ontario, where I grew up in the 1940s and '50s, most men were fathers, most women were mothers, and everyone else was "eccentric." The same was true when we moved to Toronto's suburbs in the late 1950s and early 1960s. The rules were the same for all, and we thought that, in all the essentials, we were pretty much the same.

When I look at the fifty-year-old guys in my life and in my surveys today, I may see the demographic stereotype. But I am just as likely to see the exceptions to the rule. I see fifty-year-old men who are grandfathers. I see fifty-year-old men who are fathers of children ranging in age from newborn to thirty or even older, often with at least one ex-wife and/or one common-law partner thrown into the mix. Some are ending their careers and thinking about retirement and lowering their golf handicap. Others are starting new careers, ventures or projects, still eager to take a few risks and maybe make a difference.

And here I am only pointing to the obvious demographic diversity. Think of the even greater diversity in the character, motivations and personality of people you know who are the same age. Think for a moment of the incredible diversity of perspectives in this most multicultural of countries. When you add "psychographic" diversity to demographic diversity, you have a country in which no single group is either dominant or archetypal.

Go to lunch in a private club in Montreal, Toronto or Vancouver, and then take a ride on the Métro/subway or a walk around Stanley Park. The contrast between the tired ethnic homogeneity of an aging and evanescent élite, and the vitality and diversity in the wider society is breathtaking.

It is true there have always been outsiders and eccentrics: "spinster" aunts, "queer old men," "Jews," "coloured folk," the handicapped. Today, however, these "minorities," and a myriad of others, are more likely to be mainstream. This is because *everyone* is now an outsider or eccentric in some sense, even though the poor, people of colour, the mentally and physically disabled and natives are still more "outside" than others. The stereotypes often no longer exist, or when they do, they join the parade of all other minorities. White, Anglo-Saxon men who believe in God, the monarch, and the "golden rule" — soon to be displayed in a museum near you, in the diorama next to the dinosaur exhibit.

I grew up in a Canada where leaders led and followers followed, where there was a place for everyone, and everyone knew his or her place. Canadians were categorized by such variables as who their parents were, their religion, their age, gender and family status — father, mother, grandparent, child — and by their race or ethnic background. All

too often, these labels became epithets used to differenti-
ate and then to segregate. Today, these categories are
becoming less relevant as Canadians eschew the societally
imposed stereotypes of the past. More and more,
Canadians refuse to be constrained by the specifics of their
demographics; instead, they are determined to be the
authors of their own identities and destinies. They demand
to exercise individual choice and personal control over who
they are, what they do and who they will be, and finally,
with whom they will have their most intimate, meaningful
— and sometimes not so meaningful — relationships.

Canadians have done this by rejecting the power of traditional institutional authorities, whether they be religious or
secular. At the ballot box, they began to question the legitimacy of the gerontocracy that had managed Canada since
before Confederation. And, this general questioning of
"men in suits" also took place at work, in the community
and in the home. The kind of authority that gains respect
today is not based on fear, intimidation or guilt, but is more
voluntaristic and consensual. Not chiselled in marble, but
flexible. Not based on relationships in a rigid hierarchy, but
fluid, plastic and more authentic.

This book hopes to portray the diversity of the Canadian
character in a way that has not been done before. It is a
psychographic geography of Canada. *Sex in the Snow* is
based on in-depth surveys of Canadians' social values, scientific investigations of the underlying motivations that propel our culture. In my opinion, this research reveals much

more than the "mood of the nation" polls that often show Canadians euphoric one year and catatonic the next. The real story is much more complicated.

In these pages I tell the story of what I see as the evolution of the Canadian character, and some ideas about what we may expect in the future, when the baby boomers are displaced by Generation X and its successors. What sort of society will Canada be when traditional institutions wield even less authority than they do now over the lives of Canadians? What about the future of our nation? Can we hope to remain a distinct sub-culture on this continent?

Will Canada be the utopia of peace, order and good government promised in our 1867 constitution? Or will it evolve into the dystopia of narcissism and social Darwinism we Canadians see in the republic to the south? What are the prospects for the Canadian character in the century ahead?

As I see it, some institutions will decline, some will be invented, others, like government, will be reinvented. Those in decline, like organized religion, will leave their vestigial remnants, like the pyramids in Egypt and Chartres Cathedral in France, as three-star destinations for tomorrow's tourists. Some institutions will adapt to change, but *none* will last a thousand years, and none will dominate our culture like the church, state and corporate monopolies did in the past. Too many people have too much freedom to sustain the dominance of such authoritarian institutions. The old monoliths are being replaced by a plethora of new institutions, organizations and networks that enable people to achieve the fundamental values now energizing our civilization: autonomy, hedonism and a quest for meaning.

I believe that the institutional changes that are taking place in this country, and Canadians' reactions to them, cannot be fully appreciated without an understanding of changes in Canadians' underlying, and evolving, social values. Of course, the relationship between institutions and social values is a two-way street. The social values of Canadians are reflected in the institutions they have created for themselves. These structures, in their turn, have contributed to the development of a distinctly Canadian world-view. Though the crisis of declining confidence in traditional institutions is now being experienced by many countries around the world, it is almost palpable here, for a number of reasons.

First of all, many Canadians relied upon — and to a lesser extent, continue to rely upon — a highly interventionist government that promises to look after them, come hell or high water. Well, hell has come, in the form of fiscal limitations on our public sector, and fierce global competition in the private marketplace. Unfortunately, many Canadians failed to don their asbestos suits and strap a lemonade tank on their backs. Naturally, the pain they're now experiencing lessens their confidence in their political leaders and institutions.

In addition, Canadians are now forming new attachments

with a diversity of communities, within *and* without Canada. These include the new on-line communities that disregard national borders and individual stereotypes. Canadians' enthusiasm for these new technologies, and their growing ability to form their own networks rather than rely on historical institutions, is contributing to the "values tribalization" of the country. Once defined by our race, religion or region, now we define ourselves by our values, by our personal priorities and by our life choices.

What follows is my view of Canada's evolution from an industrial nation-state to a post-industrial, post-modern community, and my analysis of the values tribes which will shape our destiny.

1

DEMOGRAPHY IS NOT DESTINY

"Life was charmed, but without politics or religion. It was the life of children of the children of the pioneers — life after God — a life of earthly salvation on the edge of heaven."

— Douglas Coupland, *Life After God*

In his book *Life After God*, Douglas Coupland muses on the possibilities and meaning of an existence without a Supreme Being. He tries to be hopeful, but, at the same time, expresses uncertainty. I have chosen the above quotation because I believe, beyond doubt, that we can live quite happily in a secular world. But that is not to say, a world without meaning.

Is it possible that we in Canada have nearly achieved this "life of earthly salvation on the edge of heaven"? According to the UN at least, we've succeeded in achieving the highest quality of life in the world. Our geography, size and history of accommodation of different groups has resulted in a more affluent and egalitarian society. Ideologically, we are

a serendipitous mixture of toryism, liberalism and socialism. Personally, I believe that our success as a nation is
also due, in part, to the declining influence of traditional
demographic characteristics in defining this country and its
people. We are creating a new post-modern Canadian culture.

To some, it may seem counter-intuitive to assert that
demography is losing its potency as a determinant of life's
chances, at a time when ethnic strife around the world has
entire populations in the grip of fear and hatred, when ethnic nationalism threatens the continued existence of our
own country, and when, on the surface, our multicultural
reality makes us look more different from one another, and
see many of our political conflicts through the outdated
prism of ethnic rivalries. However, if there is anything quintessentially "Canadian" about our culture, it is precisely the
declining influence of demographic characteristics in determining our world-views and opportunities. This, and the
waning power of traditional institutions, is creating a very
different Canada from that of even the fairly recent past.

Institutional authority has been increasingly scrutinized and
questioned, not only in Canada, but around the world.
However, as a result of our unique historical, geographical
and cultural context, the critique here has taken a distinct
form. Canadians have had a tradition of valuing "peace,
order and good government." Though many now see "good
government" as an oxymoron, they continue to cherish
ideals of peace and order. Moreover, this cynicism toward

governments and institutions has not made Canadians any less political. Rather, the macro-politics of institutions is being eclipsed by the micro-politics of personal networks, both present and virtual.

A micro-political quest for equality continues on all fronts: between spouses and between children of all ages and their parents; between friends; between colleagues at work; between strangers meeting on the street, or surfing on the Internet. The formal conventions and structures that shaped our orientations to others are quickly being replaced by informality and flexibility. Constitutions and the laws of parliament are less relevant because they can no longer regulate the voluntary flows of goods, services and information that give substance and meaning to Canadians in their day-to-day lives.

About a decade ago, French philosopher Régis Debray observed that there is more power in rock 'n' roll than in all the armies of Russia. Before the Berlin Wall fell in 1989, that barricade was a universal symbol of totalitarian authority. Our version of that Wall is the complex network of anachronistic institutions that support hierarchy, patriarchy and role stereotypes based on age, gender, race, ethnicity and other arbitrary demographic characteristics. Now, Berlin Walls are falling every day in Canada as yet another "minority" asserts its autonomy and its right to hedonistic pleasure and the quest for a more meaningful life.

demography is not destiny

Breathtaking social change has taken place in the space of a single generation, and a population whose personality was unidimensional has become multidimensional. By this, I do not mean that we don't value our identities as men or women, as young, middle-aged or old, or as someone with definable ethnic or cultural roots. In fact, most of us are proud of these elements and, in many ways, savour and rediscover aspects of our identity as they become more important to us at various times in our life. What I am saying is that we are no longer willing to be the prisoner of any one identity, but rather, opt for a flexibility of self-definition that can be adjusted by the individual, depending on the situation or circumstance.

Until recently, demography *was* destiny. Now, we transcend the societal stereotypes — male/female, young/old, French/English, Catholic/Protestant, black/white, straight/gay — to fashion new personal images and identities. In a single generation, the Canadian family has been redefined, with common-law and same-sex relationships enjoying greater recognition, and women having attained opportunities to leave the home and aspire to success in professions previously reserved almost exclusively for men.

Today, like many fathers, I aspire no less for my daughter than for my son and vice versa. Not too long ago, girls thought of their futures largely in terms of being housewives, or nurses, schoolteachers or social workers. Now the sexual, ethnic and other demographic ghettos have been blasted open. In many respects, society is still not egalitarian. But, if I am right, we will never return to the stereotypes of the past, stereotypes that prevented so many from asserting their autonomy, enjoying a wide range of experiences, and searching for greater personal meaning in their lives.

How did this happen? To give a summary of what were, in fact, complex social forces, I like to go back to April 1966, and *Time* magazine's provocative cover story, which posed the question "Is God Dead?" Of course, the German philosopher Friedrich Nietzsche and others had covered this story a century earlier, and the philosophical question of God's mortality is really a more fit subject for theologians and philosophers than pollsters. However, the sociological meaning of God's retreat, especially in Canada, is one that twenty-five years of polling research has inspired me to address. Moreover, it is a subject that has not been widely discussed, at least by Canadian writers of non-fiction.

Weekly attendance has been declining steadily in places of worship in Canada for several decades now. In the late 1940s, 60 per cent of Canadians reported attending church services weekly. By the mid-1960s, however, the first baby boomers were reaching maturity and starting to question — and then reject — religious authority and ritual practices in numbers never before seen. By 1996, regular church attendance stood at 30 per cent, and only 21 per cent among Canadians under thirty.[3] Though most Canadians — 83 per cent — still say they believe in God, the proportion of Canadians who identify with a religion continues to decline, and a record number of Canadians say they have no religious affiliation.

Increasingly, Canadians are giving up on traditional religious dogma in favour of a less guilt-ridden spirituality. Growing numbers of hedonistic and experience-seeking Canadians reject the existence of a devil or Hell. This leads me to conclude that, if exorcising guilt was the main motivation, maybe *Time* got it wrong — perhaps it's the Devil who is dead, and we have become God. Sex in the snow, complete with snow angels.

In many ways, it is this "death of the Devil" that heralded the erosion of Canadians' Judeo-Christian view of the universe. Fear and guilt were often the greatest factors sustaining church-attendance numbers, and motivating Canadians to behave according to the dictates of religious strictures. These emotions are still major motivators among many older Canadians, and even among some baby boomers. But among younger Canadians, they are dying, along with the Judeo-Christian dogma that supported them.

It seems to me as a researcher — and as a baby boomer who went through the process of youthful rebellion — that the symbolism of "killing" God — and the Devil — was important for boomers and the culture they were about to dominate. After killing the One True God, and thereby risking the fate of eternal damnation in the fires of hell, the slaying of lesser gods — including any once-unquestioned authorities — became much less intimidating, if not inevitable.

sex in the snow

I was raised as a Roman Catholic. I remember, as if it were yesterday, my mother kneeling before the altar in Sacred Heart Church in Walkerton, Ontario, on my first day of school, praying for her little boy. I was soon to be an acolyte, and dutifully went to mass and communion on nine successive first Fridays of the month, thus ensuring I would never die in a state of mortal sin and suffer the fires of everlasting hell. Then, at the age of fourteen, I took my first step toward the kind of critical world-view that has shaped and sustained me as an adult. I told our parish priest that I had read a story in *The Toronto Star* about the population explosion, and asked how the Pope could oppose artificial birth control in the face of this crisis. He looked down at me, literally and figuratively, and answered me rhetorically in precisely these words: "Do you think God is stupid?" I had no answer, then. Perhaps, thirty-six years later, this book is my reply.

After "killing" God, one by one we "killed" all the "fathers" in our lives, whether they sat across from us at the dinner table, stood at the front of our classrooms, signed our pay cheques or determined the religious and secular laws that governed our lives. Within five years of confronting my parish priest in Rexdale, I found myself in Ottawa, a student delegate from Queen's University at the famous 1966 annual meeting of the Progressive Conservative party. I cheered on my hero, Dalton Camp, the incumbent party president who was running for re-election on a platform of the need to review the leadership of none other than the Rt. Hon. John George Diefenbaker — the man who had led the federal Tories out of the political wilderness and into power less than a decade before. My iconoclasm had quite naturally evolved from sacred to secular idols, and I was neither alone nor, as a young "red Tory," among the most radical of my generation.

In some ways the death of God, which I found personally liberating, also signalled the beginning of the end for patriarchy in popular consciousness, and the start of the feminist revolution. Much of the credit for women's growing equality in family and professional life must also go to women who came of age in the 1970s — not just the early bra-burners, but those formidable young women who quietly took advantage of their growing reproductive freedom to expand their personal and professional horizons. The doors of "the white men's club" were thrown open. The girls joined the party in the wake of the Pill, as did visible minorities in the wake of Martin Luther King, Jr. and the Black Panthers.

Questioning "Dad" made it much easier for boomers to question the authority of teachers, doctors, bosses, politicians and the so-called élites. Among approximately eighty trends tracked by the 3SC Social Values Monitor, those of particular importance to boomers are *Rejection of Authority*, *Rejection of Order*, *Control of Destiny*, *Pursuit of Happiness to the Detriment of Duty* and *Equality of the Sexes*. As these labels imply, these values measure Canadians' desire to "grab life by the collar," to assert control and to enjoy life today rather than wait for some distant tomorrow.

sex in the snow

In previous centuries, values tended to get passed from one generation to the next. However, the sheer numerical preponderance of boomers in the population, and the appeal of their values, broke this pattern. Over the past quarter century, we have seen the values of boomers passed, not just to younger generations, but also into the consciousness of the older ones too.

The boomers cannot take sole credit, however, for the modernization of values in Canada. Our social-values research shows that there is a small but extremely important group of older Canadians who preceded the boomers in questioning the status quo, and who significantly paved the way for the rebellious generation that followed. We have called them the Cosmopolitan Modernists. In Quebec, they led the Quiet Revolution in the 1950s and '60s — Pierre Trudeau, Jean Marchand, René Lévesque and their confrères. In English Canada, they were instrumental in bringing the country's academic and governmental institutions into the twentieth century, thereby building the magnificent edifice of the Canadian social welfare state. People like former provincial premiers William Davis, Allan Blakeney and Peter Lougheed; senior government mandarins like Lester Pearson, Robert Bryce and Gordon Robertson. These people were, to borrow David Halberstam's felicitous phrase, "the best and the brightest" of their generation.

Affluence, education, travel and the mass media inspired boomers to become much more nomadic than their parents. They visited places that, prior to the 1960s, few Canadians had ever seen. And even when their bodies weren't travelling, their minds were being transported to exotic venues in the global village of television.

Of course, not everyone has celebrated the baby-boomer legacy in our culture. Many boomers accepted their parents' values wholeheartedly. The critics of our post-modern culture see it as poor, narcissistic, trivial and ultimately meaningless. They believe there are no more great ideas, nor great men to advance them, only "empowered" consumers in a futile quest for the god they abandoned in pursuit of the good life in shopping centres and television sitcoms.

Whether the present democratized culture is an improvement or a degradation is open to debate. What *is* clear, however, is that the opinions and attitudes of the general population are more important than ever before, for the simple reason that the viewpoint and the expertise of our putative élites matter less and less. I believe that by the year 2020, the institutions the boomers fought to reform will have much less significance for Generations X, Y and Z. Organized religion, institutions like universities, the professions and yes, even the nation-state — all will be much less relevant. I make this prediction on the basis of my reading of current trends in economics, politics and technology, and in light of the evolving social values of Canadians.

Sophisticated multivariate computer analysis, or "cluster analysis," suggests that previous generations were characterized by a degree of social cohesion, conformity and consensus that is now breaking down. When Canadians are divided according to their social values, twelve groups emerge: three groups among Canadians fifty years of age or older; four groups among the baby boomers, and five groups among the post-boomers. This finding is significant, because it confirms that younger Canadians, though smaller in numbers than boomers or older Canadians, divide into more social values "tribes" than do their predecessors.

The same analysis shows that consensus on social values is determined less and less by demographic factors. Among older Canadians, differences in social values are largely determined by differences in such demographic variables as gender, education and income, but this is less true among younger groups. I believe that the media-rich environment in which we live is making it easier for people to construct for themselves sets of values that are not limited by personal demographic characteristics. This, I believe, is a sociological finding of seminal importance. *Demography is no longer destiny.*

Even the great divide between English- and French-speaking Canadians conforms to my conclusion. While not wishing to belittle the values differences that separate the two linguistic "solitudes" of Canada, we have found that far greater divisions exist among the generations than between anglophones and francophones. Generally, those over fifty want to restore our institutions; the boomers want to reform them, and Generation X is pretty much ready to write them off as irrelevant. If there are in fact two solitudes in Canada, they are the young and the old.

When Nietzsche announced the death of God, the majority of people still believed in the existence of a Supreme Being. His point, however, was not so much that there is no God, but rather that a certain way of looking at the world, formerly taken for granted by almost everyone, had been thrown into question. The death of God meant the death of a world-view predicated on the devaluation of the physical world, the attribution of metaphysical significance to natural phenomena, and the inculcation of guilt and duty as fundamental motives for people.

The death of God — or, as I suggested earlier, of the Devil — has resulted in a population that is unwilling to defer gratification to the next life, that wants to "have its cake and eat it too." What is the point, after all, of having a cake you don't eat, or waiting till it's stale? Canadians are increasingly focused on immediate gratification, and have pretty much given up on the promises — and *threats* — of an afterlife.

In Canada, this death of the Devil is accompanied by the first significant signs of the declining influence of demography. As is the case of religious belief, many people still identify themselves and pigeon-hole others primarily in terms of their sex, age and race. And with older Canadians, demographic differences are often strong predictors of social values. However, these factors are becoming less significant in determining the actual social values and lifestyles of Canadians, especially younger Canadians. This distinguishes the cultural evolution in Canada from that observed in the United States, where demographic factors, especially race, still remain more obvious determinants of values, lifestyles and opportunities.

We are living at a time when history and geography are compressed. The pace of change seems permanently stuck on "fast forward," and there is a growing awareness of the interconnectedness of people and events around the world. Changes that used to take decades happen now in years or even months. As a result of advances in communication technologies, "nomads" are no longer simply those who move physically from place to place, but also those who travel *virtually*, creating networks, projects and communities with people they have never met, who live in places they may never visit. Thanks to virtual travel through the globalization of culture, teenagers in Toronto, Miami and Kiev often have more in common with each other than they do with their own parents.

The truth of this assertion was made palpably vivid for me in 1987 when travelling with friends in the former Soviet Union. After a day of tourism in Kiev, we took a walk in a park near our hotel and discovered a *Komsomol* (Communist League of Youth) centre. The kids we met were not imbibing Marxist ideology, but rather, rock 'n' roll hits such as Madonna's then-current "Papa Don't Preach." A young man named Vladimir, whose nickname was "Bob," bragged about his knowledge of American slang, and asked us what we thought of Glass Tiger, then Canada's top rock band. Is it any wonder the Berlin Wall fell three years later, with the authorities relying on young men like Bob to prop it up?

Of course, here in Canada teenagers and their parents both face the retreat of government from its historic roles. However, in the wake of the withdrawal of government from individuals' lives, and the twilight of religious and secular idols, the response from Canadians has been neither anarchy nor nihilism. Rather, we find a growing sense of interconnectedness and personal empowerment. We are also witnessing the development of a particularly "Canadian" pragmatism and adaptability, a *calculus of contingency* in a world in which any secular or religious ideology seems implausible, unappealing or even evil. Such a calculus aims to maximize hedonistic pleasure in the short term, while balancing long-term relationships, commitments and costs. This is the way we now behave at home, at work, and in the political and consumer marketplaces. In Canada, at the end of the millennium, the communities of the past, based on family, church and state are discarded (as in the case of the church), discredited (as in the case of the state) or modified to accommodate diversity (as in the case of the family). At the same time, values tribalism and new types of communities, such as the virtual communities of the Internet, grow exponentially.

sex in the snow

My generation, the baby boomers, marked a transition from the communitarian or community-centred values of the 1950s to the values of liberal individualism. The post-boomer generation, Generation X, is now blazing trails from individualism to a sort of post-individualism in which experience-seeking connections are more important than the mere assertion of autonomy and personal control.

New values and motivations are developing in our culture that are anything but traditional, and go well beyond the often egocentric self-fulfilment espoused by the baby boomers. New trends that emerged in the 1980s are cen-tred on such concepts as *polysensualism*, *intuitive potential*, *interest in the mysterious*, *vitality*, *flexibility of personality* and *flexibility of gender identity*. In the 1990s, these currents are realized in the context of a renewed interest in technol-ogy, networking and a quest for meaning.

A new social fabric of communities is now being woven on the basis of values rather than on the basis of ethnic or demographic identities. *I am connected with my family and my ethnic tribe, but on my own terms and not uncritically. I connect with strangers through technology, networks and participation in mass events.* It is this sort of cosmopoli-tanism that has allowed our largest city, Toronto, to become one of the most multicultural metropolises in the world.

The boomers' legacy was to promote the widespread acceptance of individual autonomy, the most visible symbol of which is Pierre Trudeau's 1982 Charter of (individual) Rights and Freedoms. The movement to post-individualism does not mean a regression to the ethnic tribalism of the past, but rather, a progression to communities of choice based on mutual interest, affinity and need, as well as greater flexibility of personality, and even of race and gender identity. What I am talking about here goes beyond the strategic selection of different faces for different places — the guy, for instance, who is subservient to his boss, but a dictator to his wife and children. It's the evocation of different personalities within oneself as a way of playing with a reality that is seen as fluid rather than static.

One of the most perceptive analyses of the way this type of exploration is carried out on the Internet is that presented by cyberspace sociologist Sherry Turkle in her book *Life on the Screen: Identity in the Age of the Internet*.[4] Ms. Turkle talks about the way in which people use MUDS (multi-user domains) to test different identities, try on different roles, and explore new aspects of their personalities. MUD players surf the MUD sites under the guise of any number of different personae, all of their own invention. One man, for instance, played four different characters — a seductive woman, a macho cowboy, a passive rabbit of undetermined gender and a sexual tourist — on three different sites. Another player, a woman, dealt with the trauma of losing her leg in an automobile accident by creating a character with a similar affliction and allowing that character to come to terms with the amputation, and even take a virtual lover.

Ms. Turkle describes how these MUDs allow people "to develop ideas about identity as multiplicity." In traditional societies, where institutions, symbols and relationships are stable, the self is seen as unitary. People are encouraged to think of themselves as a One: a woman was never to hear certain language, for example, or a man would think of himself as "the boss," whether at work or at home. However, as traditional institutions, symbols and relationships break down, and society is recognized as being in flux, the idea of the One unitary core is forced to give way. Instead, the healthy personality must develop the flexibility to negotiate through many identities. This new psychological and philosophical model of self emphasizes fluidity and multiplicity.

This is reflected among many younger Canadians, among whom there is now a new flexibility of personality — even a sort of playfulness — formerly only dreamt of by poets, and only realized by creative eccentrics like Oscar Wilde, T. E. Lawrence (of Arabia) and Virginia Woolf. Today, many more people have the opportunity to explore their "other selves." And why not? God is dead, the King is dead and Daddy is dead, for I can be God, King, Daddy and anything else I choose. Is this megalomania? No. Rather, it is the type of "healthy multiple personalities" Sherry Turkle talks about in her work.

Imagination has always played a role in constructing people's identities. There have always been people who have expressed different facets of their personality, depending on the situation. In recent history, however, this phe-

nomenon has made a quantum leap to new possibilities. A
hundred years ago, for instance, the average woman was
too tired by the end of the day to do much more than sleep,
and her identity was essentially limited to her status in the
family and the religion her father had chosen. For her, biol-
ogy and demography were destiny. Today, an increase in
available income, leisure time and communication media
have conspired to present people with an unprecedented
selection of ideas, fashions, images and role models from
which to construct and reconstruct their own identity. In
the past people in similar occupational situations could be
expected to harbour similar views on many of the important
questions of the day. Today, such an assumption is precar-
ious indeed. For Canadians at least, demography is no
longer destiny, and their social values no longer simply
reflect the ethnic, regional and occupational groups to
which they belong.

*If I am not living a life of self-sacrifice and gratification
deferred to the next life, then I want to cram as much experience as I can into the cosmic second I am allotted in this life.
How? By giving expression to as many aspects of my personality as possible. I am at once male and female, young
and old, universal and particular. I can be strong ("male") at
the office and nurturing ("female") at home, or vice versa. I
can be a mature adult and occasionally a crazy, carefree
teenager. I can lead or I can follow — depending on my com-
petence, interest and circumstances — what we label the
transition from hierarchy to heterarchy. I can be a member
of an élite in one sphere, but just an ordinary guy in many*

others. And unlike in the past, I DECIDE. My behaviour is not dictated by historical precedent or societal conventions. All this is the personality equivalent of digital compression: multiple signals in one channel, multiple identities in one life.

Another expression of this trend toward a more flexible definition of self is the phenomenon of teenagers of all races appropriating the rap culture originated by inner-city blacks. They have seized the music and attire of a cultural group with which, on the surface at least, they have little in common. The rap singer Snow is a good example of this phenomenon. Is an Irish-Canadian who speaks Jamaican, dresses Jamaican, dances Jamaican and gesticulates Jamaican still Irish-Canadian in any but the most trivial sense? Another example of the dissolution of static identities is Alanis Morissette's simultaneously aggressive and vulnerable image as she sings to a boyfriend who has left her for another woman, "Is she perverted like me? Would she go down on you in a theatre?" So, too, is k.d. lang's gender-bending iconoclasm. Aural sex in the snow.

My own anecdotal evidence supports the dissolution of traditional gender roles. My five-year-old daughter, Marion, is very physical, and in the past would have been singled out as a "tomboy." But the fact is, many of her little girlfriends don't seem much different. And to complete the portrait of role reversal, my two-year-old son, William, is happiest when he is vacuuming the house.

The development of flexible identities is being spearheaded

by young Canadians. Like the values of the baby boomers, their values will be exported to the wider society, and perhaps, by the millennium, the boomers will get over the shock of realizing they are no longer the sole source of novelty in the cultural universe. Despite their smaller numbers, young Canadians' greater mastery of new information and communication technologies will facilitate their influence on us all. Though demographically disadvantaged at the ballot box, young Canadians are at a distinct advantage where it increasingly counts: in front of a personal computer and on-line, where personal identities achieve a new dimension of fluidity.

Having discarded, in large measure, their traditional attachments to religious and secular faiths, Canadians have constructed a national identity that consists of flexible, multiple personalities — a sort of synergistic schizophrenia. And although Canadians continue to value their individual linguistic and ethnic roots, fewer and fewer remain prisoners of any one identity that dictates their every thought and action. And, in many ways, this growing complexity applies even more to Canadians in Quebec than to those in the rest of the country — a significant fact that is often overlooked because of the ethnic tribalism that dominates politics in that province. In Quebec, the political dialectic tends to disguise the growing complexity in the character of francophone Quebecers.

The constitutional debate focuses on Quebec's aspirations for recognition as a "distinct society" and its quest for powers to preserve its language and culture. But the reality is that more and more Quebecers, both anglophones and francophones, are bilingual, as well as being exposed on a daily basis to American popular culture. Bilingual Canadians are among the most modern in their world-views, and tend to be more focused on freedom, personal fulfilment and experience-seeking than are their unilingual peers. In many ways, they combine the best aspects of both cultures. Their ability to communicate in different languages is a passport to post-modernity.

It must be acknowledged that there *are* differences in values between the so-called English-Canadian and French-Canadian personalities that have persisted over time. The French are more social in their orientation; the English are more individualistic. The French are more likely to emphasize passion, appearance and symbolism or what the Italians call *la bella figura*. This made the scenario in Jean-Claude Lauzon's film *Léolo*, in which a young Québécois fantasizes that he is Italian, particularly plausible. The English, on the other hand, emphasize what they think of as "concrete" or "substantive." However, despite these differences, our research shows that the values gap between francophones and anglophones is much smaller than is commonly supposed, and certainly smaller than at the time of Confederation or even twenty-five years ago. Overall basic values do not separate French and English Canadians, nor does the context in which we find ourselves: that is, the globalization of trade, finance, technology and culture, or the crushing burden of our public debt.

demography is not destiny

Ironically, as French and English Canadians become more similar over time, to some people the differences that remain can seem more important. This is a phenomenon that Sigmund Freud called the "narcissism of small differences." A century ago, French and English Canadians were very different on a range of dimensions, including religion, family size and occupation. Today, language remains one of Quebec's few defining characteristics. No wonder many French Quebecers respond to globalizing trends by asserting their distinctiveness, even though, in the larger context, we are all evolving into the post-modern multiple-identity consciousness that will define Canadians in the millennium ahead.

2

CANADIAN GENERATIONS: NOT BACK TO THE FUTURE

"The place they had chosen to come, to be their best selves, to be unconscious of ancestry. Here, apart from the sun compass and the odometer mileage and the book, he was alone, his own invention."

— Michael Ondaatje, *The English Patient*

Historically, one generation usually passed its values on to the next, which then did its best to maintain and build upon those cultural traditions. However, at various times in history, economic and technological change have interrupted this continuity, sometimes with revolutionary conse- quences. The Italian Renaissance in the fifteenth century, America in 1776, France in 1789, Russia in 1917 —all examples of history at the crossroads, at what have been referred to as "liminal moments" when old structures have been dismantled and the new is in the process of being created, with little regard for the recent past. These have been times of great creativity, and also of great personal stress.

Canada, and other Euro-American societies, experienced a social revolution in the 1960s. Rebellious ideas, spawned in the conformist 1950s, inspired and informed a "counter-cultural" revolution in that tumultuous decade that was shaped by the vanguard of the postwar baby boomers. This was the era when everything seemed to be up for grabs. Many people, but especially the young, questioned traditional religious authority. There was a wholesale redefinition of the roles of women and the status of racial and ethnic minorities. The music changed, literally and figuratively.

This break with tradition inspired social scientists like Alain de Vulpian in France, and Daniel Yankelovich in the United States, to analyze, document and track the changes transforming the socio-cultural dynamics in their societies. These researchers identified the new orientation to hedonism and self-fulfilment in Euro-American cultures. What has yet to be documented, in my opinion, is the evolution of social values that transpired in the *Canadian* context since the cultural revolution of the 1960s, and that will help shape this country in the early decades of the next millennium.

Several years ago, the social-values research my company had been doing led me to speculate that, increasingly, Canadians were undergoing the personality equivalent of digital compression. The decline of guilt, *noblesse oblige* and the Judeo-Christian code of duty had created a culture that ceased to defer gratification to the next life, or even till old age. The entire focus became *this* life, here and now. Heaven on earth, rather than earth as a mere antechamber for the hereafter. A host of new experience-seeking values — for example, *flexibility of personality*, *sensualism*, *vitality*, *adaptive navigation* and *flexibility of gender identity* — seemed to be evidence of a society wishing to compress as much experience as possible into the seven or eight decades most of us are allotted.

I saw growing evidence of this wish to cram as much experience as possible into one's life, including the experiences of people living in different regions, local or global, and even people of different sexes and races. My colleagues and I speculated that this desire, combined with a media-rich environment that allows people to construct their own idiosyncratic world-views from an ever-expanding range of sources, might result in the decreasing importance of demographics in determining Canadians' social values and behaviour. To test this hypothesis, we looked at our social-values data in a slightly different way, in what is known as a "cluster analysis." Let me now briefly explain the methodology behind the research in this book.

In the socio-cultural research my company conducts, the values of Canadians are explored through the measurement of a number of trends plotted on a socio-cultural "map." The construction of this map is a multi-stage statistical process, using as its raw material the approximately 2,600 interviews we conduct annually as part of our 3SC Social Values Monitor.

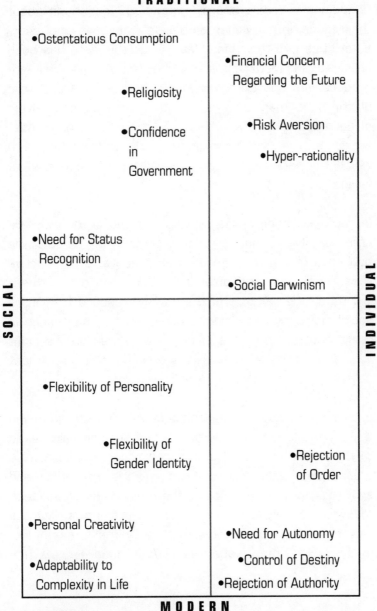

Position of Selected Trends on the Socio-Cultural Map   3SC

TRADITIONAL

•Ostentatious Consumption

•Financial Concern
Regarding the Future

•Religiosity

•Risk Aversion

•Confidence
in
Government

•Hyper-rationality

•Need for Status
Recognition

•Social Darwinism

SOCIAL

INDIVIDUAL

•Flexibility of Personality

•Flexibility of
Gender Identity

•Rejection
of Order

•Personal Creativity

•Need for Autonomy

•Control of Destiny

•Adaptability to
Complexity in Life

•Rejection of Authority

MODERN

Environics

In each of these surveys, a representative sample of Canadians is asked approximately 250 questions about their fundamental values or beliefs, their personal characteristics and their lifestyles. Once this data has been collected, and factor analyses completed, the questions are grouped into approximately 80 "trends." The trends are placed on a "map" using a method called "factor analysis of correspondence." In this way, the values (or trends) appear on the map in proximity to the other values with which they are most highly correlated, in "clusters" of values.

In general, trends appearing near the top of the map are correlated with a more traditional world-view. Those at the bottom reflect a more modern perspective, a perspective that questions, and often rejects, traditional values. Trends on the left side of the map correspond to a more social orientation to life (one's cues tend to be defined in relation to the opinions of others). Those on the right reflect a more individualistic stance (in which the most salient factor is one's own point of view, not others').

Examining the map more closely, we see that the trends in the upper-left *"Traditional-Social"* quadrant generally relate to the desire for social status and success, and revolve around the idea of traditional communities, institutions and social recognition. Trends in the upper-right *"Traditional-Individual"* quadrant tend to relate to a focus on financial independence, and security and stability in all areas of life. In the lower-right *"Modern-Individual"* quadrant, we find trends related to personal freedom, fulfilment and autonomy. In the lower-left *"Modern-Social"* quadrant, we find experience-seeking trends built around the desire for exploration, adventure and novelty, as well as trends reflecting an interest in new communities, such as those found on the Internet.

TRADITIONAL

SOCIAL

INDIVIDUAL

Traditional Communities, Institutions and Social Status

Financial Independence, Stability and Security

Experience-seeking and New Communities

Personal Autonomy and Self-Fulfilment

MODERN

Environics

If the so-called "average Canadian" were placed on the map, he or she would be found at the intersection of the two axes on the map. As Canadians have generally moved to a more individualistic, less social posture over the past fifteen years, this intersection has moved somewhat to the right (toward the *Individual* pole) and slightly down (toward the *Modern* pole). As we look at Canadians, we find that those who are more traditional in their answers will be higher on the map, those who are more modern will be lower. Canadians who are more social will be further to the left; those who are more individualistic will be further to the right. By analyzing a respondent's answers to all of the social-values questions on the survey, we can create a synthesis map for a single individual. That individual will appear as a single dot on the map, placed according to whether her/his values are Traditional or Modern (and to what degree) and Social or Individual (and to what degree). This dot will then be grouped together with the dots closest to it to identify a cluster of individuals sharing similar values, or what we call a "values tribe." (Readers who wish to have a little fun with our 3SC social values system are invited to visit the Environics Internet site — http://www.environics.net — where you will have the chance to answer a short form of our questionnaire, and then see where our computer places you on the socio-cultural map.)

The Evolution of Canadian Values
3SC Canada 1983–Present

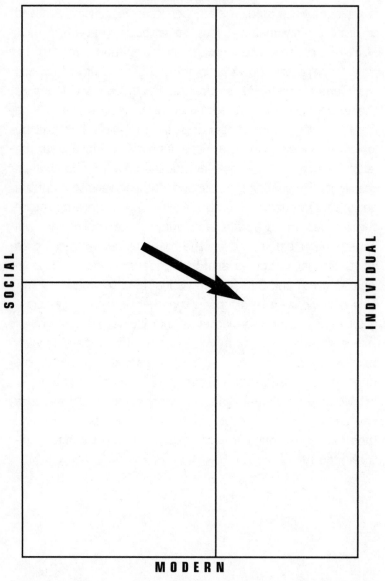

TRADITIONAL

SOCIAL

INDIVIDUAL

MODERN

Environics

To test the hypothesis that society was becoming more complex, and that this complexity would be translated into a greater diversity of socio-cultural segments or "values tribes," we divided the population into three broad age groups: the pre-boomers (those aged fifty or over in 1995); the baby boomers (those aged thirty to forty-nine); and Generation X (those aged fifteen to twenty-nine). Though the characters in Douglas Coupland's eponymous novel of 1991 were in their twenties and thirties, in popular usage Generation X has come to refer to the generation that follows the boomers, so that is how I am employing the term in this book. Using the cluster of values that best reflects their world-view and lifestyles, the computer then places respondents on the socio-cultural map. The strengths of the members of various tribes on the trends (and thereby their position on the map) is determined by measuring their responses against the responses of the (mythical) "average Canadian."

At the outset, we were aware of the position on our map of the average Canadian in each of these three broad age segments, and that these average positions conformed to broad societal stereotypes of each generation: the seniors at the traditional top of the map straddling the two quadrants, with the average just inside the upper-right quadrant; the average baby boomer in the lower-right personal-freedom quadrant, and Gen X in the lower-left experience-seeking quadrant.

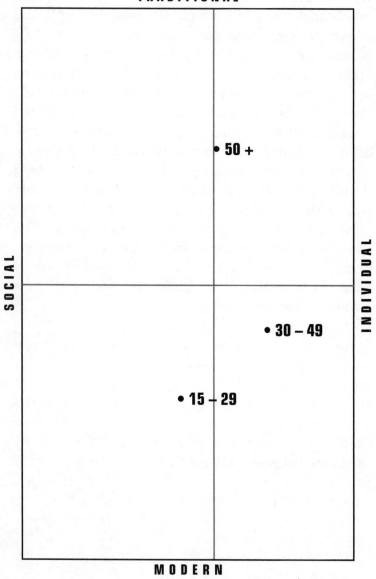

TRADITIONAL

SOCIAL

INDIVIDUAL

• 50 +

• 30 – 49

• 15 – 29

MODERN

Environics

What we didn't know yet was the degree to which the averages either reflected accurately most people in each age group, or, in fact, disguised a wide diversity within each generation. My personal hunch was that the average would be less accurate with younger groups.

Our special analysis revealed some truly remarkable findings, one of which is that the process of social fragmentation is continuing in Canada in important new ways. The much-vaunted neo-traditionalism is indeed evident in our data, but it is not the dominant trend one might expect after reading the popular press, and (incorrect) suggestions that Generation X has more in common with their grandparents than with their baby-boomer parents. Familialism, rituals, ceremonies, cigars and the martini may be back for some, or even many, but certainly not for everyone. For many on these trips back to the future, the meaning of these neo-traditional trappings has changed dramatically from what many conservatives may be seeing or hoping for.

There are twelve principal values tribes in Canada: three among those over the age of fifty, four among baby boomers, and five among those aged twenty-nine or younger (despite the fact that the last age group is the smallest in terms of population size).

My guess that there would be more diversity among the younger groups was substantiated, but we were a bit surprised to find, among those aged fifty or older, a small but very modern group that defies the stereotype, the Cosmopolitan Modernists. These people tend to be quite different from the large majority of their age peers; even we were somewhat taken aback at how different they are. We were also surprised to find that the Autonomous Rebels, who are the "defining" segment of the baby-boom generation, comprise only about one-quarter of its total. And finally, we found an even greater diversity among the youth tribes than we had anticipated; they are literally all over the map, although the average for their generation is in the lower-left ("experience-seeking," or what we jokingly refer to as the "sex, drugs and rock 'n' roll") quadrant, where one might expect to find it.

Canada's Social-Values Tribes

THE ELDERS

Rational Traditionalists	**15%**
Extroverted Traditionalists	**7%**
Cosmopolitan Modernists	**6%**

THE BOOMERS

Disengaged Darwinists	**18%**
Autonomous Rebels	**10%**
Anxious Communitarians	**9%**
Connected Enthusiasts	**6%**

GENERATION X

Aimless Dependents	**8%**
Thrill-Seeking Materialists	**7%**
Autonomous Post-Materialists	**6%**
Social Hedonists	**4%**
New Aquarians	**4%**

Environics

• **Age 15-29**   • Age 30-49   • *Age 50+*

TRADITIONAL

• *Extroverted Traditionalists (7%)*

• Anxious Communitarians (9%)

Rational •
Traditionalists (15%)

Aimless •
Dependents (8%)
Disengaged •
Darwinists (18%)

•
Thrill-seeking Materialists (7%)

SOCIAL

INDIVIDUAL

• **Social Hedonists (4%)**
• Connected
Enthusiasts (6%)

• Autonomous
Rebels (10%)

New Aquarians   *Cosmopolitan*   **Autonomous Post-**
(4%) •   *Modernists (6%) •*   **Materialists (6%) •**

Environics   **MODERN**

Our analysis also finds that, overall, women tend to be more social — and men more individualistic — in general orientation. However, the differences between the twelve values tribes are greater than the differences between the men and the women of each tribe. For example, a male Autonomous Rebel shares more values with a female Autonomous Rebel than with a male Disengaged Darwinist. The girls have not only joined the boys in almost every sphere, but the personalities of males and females are now blending in new and interesting ways. And the profiles of some of the older tribes, such as the Cosmopolitan Modernists, are closer to those of younger tribes than they are to other tribes in their own age group.

Gail Sheehy, a popular observer of social trends in the United States, believes that older baby boomers typically enter a phase in life she describes as a "second adulthood," characterized by a desire to experiment and broaden one's horizons. Our own research suggests this is not true for the "average" boomer, but that conclusion raises an important point concerning generational analysis: although age is often a factor in determining social values, increasingly of greater interest are differences in values between individuals of *similar* ages and demographic characteristics. These are the differences on which I will focus in the next three chapters.

3

THE ELDERS:
PLAYING BY THE RULES

"Canada is a country where nothing seems ever to happen.
A country always dressed in its Sunday go-to-meeting clothes.
A country you wouldn't ask to dance a second waltz. Clean.
Christian. Dull."

— Carol Shields, *The Stone Diaries*

At one time, this description of Canada's national character
was more or less accurate. There was a strong social consensus, and it was, arguably, "clean, Christian and dull."
How did we get here from there?

We start our story with Canadians fifty years of age or
older, about a third of the population (over the age of fifteen).
They were born prior to the mid-1940s. In Canada, these
are the children of the Victorians and the Edwardians. They
are people who, for the most part, accepted their parents'
values, a pattern that few of them would have questioned.
The core of these values is belief in order, authority, discipline, the Judeo-Christian moral code and the golden rule:

do unto others as you would have them do unto you. This generation lived through the most tumultuous half century since the Black Plague wiped out half of Europe's population; according to Gwynne Dyer, sixty-seven of the eighty-seven million people killed in war this century died in the first fifty years. War and the Great Depression of the 1930s left an indelible impression on the psyche of this generation. No wonder these Canadians readily accepted an absolute good versus absolute evil, black and white world-view.

When one looks at the context and events to which members of this generation were exposed, their lives seemed to be lived as the microcosm of Biblical events and prophesy, from Adam and Eve to the Apocalypse. They grew up in a world of clearly defined roles for men and women, and witnessed the mainstreaming of such inventions as the automobile, airplane, telephone and movies. And in what for many would have been their formative years, they experienced war and personal deprivation, from the dust storms of the 1930s, to the near-genocide of European Jewry in the 1940s, culminating at the end of World War II in the dawn of the nuclear era, and the threat of extinction of the entire species. Given those circumstances, even I might have hammered a few crucifixes into the wall.

Perhaps as a result of these "baptisms of fire," the world-view of these older Canadians tends to be quite clearly defined. These views are distinguished from those of younger Canadians in two fundamental ways. First, for most older Canadians, there is a right and a wrong in every area of life, from sex roles to relationships among the races, to the proper conduct of business. Second, they are willing, for the most part, to defer personal pleasure, because they believe there will be rewards in the afterlife, or because they cannot help but act upon their feelings of guilt and sense of duty.

Because material comforts could never be taken for granted, this generation put a lot of emphasis on the outward symbols of status. There was one ladder of success, and whatever rung you stood on, the symbols of achievement were almost universally understood and accepted. You start your adult life in an apartment or in your parents' home, then you buy your modest starter home, and ultimately move up to — and out into — the suburbs. As for your wheels, you start with a used Ford or Chevy, graduate to a Buick, and dream of one day driving a Cadillac.

As is often the case, the above profile is an example of an average masking important differences. When Canadians aged fifty or older are examined *en masse*, they appear to be a group with very traditional values. However, this average conceals the existence of the small but innovative and prophetic tribe, the Cosmopolitan Modernists, in addition to two other tribes, the Rational Traditionalists and the Extroverted Traditionalists. The latter two tribes, as their names suggest, tend to hold fairly traditional world-views. On the other hand, the Cosmopolitan Modernist group is composed of people who in no way resemble the archetypal anxious, conformist and risk-averse senior citizen, and who were, in my opinion, early harbingers of the Autonomous Rebels in the baby-boom generation. The two larger tribes are relatively sedentary, in the sense of being rooted in their parochial traditions; their political icons would be John Diefenbaker or Maurice Duplessis. Cosmopolitan Modernists are nomadic "citizens of the world"; their icon is former prime minister Pierre Trudeau.

These are the people who asserted their personal autonomy in the 1950s, breaking the mould of conformity when that was a much more dangerous thing to do. And in the 1960s, when the baby boomers stormed the barricades of traditional society with their revolutionary ideas and ideals, the Cosmopolitan Modernists selectively joined the party, by accepting some new mental postures such as experiential hedonism, while retaining other more traditional ones, such as a sense of duty to others.

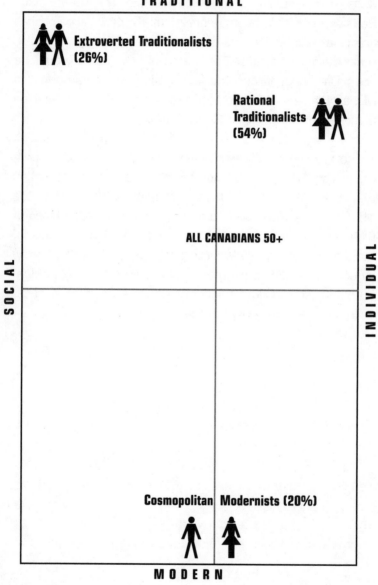

Rational Traditionalists

About half of Canadians over the age of fifty are part of the Rational Traditionalists tribe. In many ways, and especially in English Canada, members of this tribe represent the stereotypical senior citizen. A slightly higher than average proportion live in small communities of less than 5,000 people. Rational Traditionalists harbour a number of traditional values, and are in favour of the status quo, or, rather, the status quo prior to the 1960s. Clichés that typify their thinking include: "better safe than sorry"; "a bird in the hand is worth two in the bush"; "a woman's place is in the home"; "father knows best" and "beauty is only skin deep."

We have called these 3.5 million Canadians "Rational Traditionalists" because they are more likely than any other group to harbour a rational, or even hyper-rational, approach to life. To them, it is essential that emotion not cloud their considered judgment, and they take pains to ensure that this does not happen; a "stiff upper lip" in the face of adversity, for example. Accompanying this approach is an aversion to complexity, particularly the kind of social complexity associated with a multicultural society, non-traditional families, and fluidity of personality and gender identity. For example, relatively few Rational Traditionalists think Canada would be a better place if ethnic groups maintained their individual cultural identities; for most, the "melting pot" is much more appealing than the "mosaic." Very few enjoy relating to people they see as being unlike themselves. This xenophobia is closely tied to the fact that the unfamiliar and the complex are seen, not as opportunities, but as threats. Rational Traditionalists are simply not prepared to be open with strangers or to take risks, no matter what the inducement, whether that be financial gain, social status or the thrill that comes from pushing the envelope. For them, the envelope is already sealed. A few dollars on the 6/49 is about as risky as they want life to get.

Members of this group are not at ease with risk, change or the advance of technology. They give lie to the view that the more rational you are, the greater your interest in technology will be, as well as to the opinion that one cannot be rational and religious at the same time. They do not see a conflict between science and religion, because they see the two disciplines as simply dealing with different realms of experience.

Rational Traditionalists believe in traditional roles for men, women and children. They pine for the return of strong, decisive leadership in business and government, and also believe people in positions of authority should be respected by virtue of the titles they hold, even if the current crop of leaders fails to live up to the standards of real leaders like Churchill, de Gaulle and Roosevelt. They believe beyond question in the importance of honouring one's duty to others, including duties to God, country, spouse and family. Some of these people volunteered for military service during World War II, risking their lives for their ideals.

The glue binding Rational Traditionalists together is often a strong sense of guilt. Guilt has probably always been a major motivating factor in their lives, whether it be related to overt behaviour or a failure to act. Rational Traditionalists have a sense of integrity that is closely tied to their perceptions of what others expect of them and to the dictates of social conventions, and they feel badly if they do not live up to their self-imposed high standards. They are driven to be independent and self-sufficient, financially and in terms of living up to their responsibilities to others and to themselves.

Rational Traditionalists believe that traditional values survived and flourished for centuries because these values offer much in terms of structure, stability and meaning. In their minds, conformity with tradition is simply "common sense." Why should one pursue originality and novelty for their own sake? The underlying, timeless values are the ones that really count.

They are not aesthetes. In the case of people, Rational Traditionalists are more interested in "substance" than appearances, and in the case of objects, utility, not beauty, is what counts. They dismiss "political correctness," and ecological concerns as "trendy" issues that have often been blown out of all proportion. There's little chance that they would be prepared to personally pay more to protect the environment, or to boycott companies that engage in so-called "unethical" behaviour. They feel little or no guilt about this attitude because, in their opinion, threats to the environment and injustices against minorities have been exaggerated. And they are somewhat mystified that anyone would be offended by such monikers as "chair*man*" or "ladies."

Rational Traditionalists turn away *en masse* from the mysterious, the unexplained and the extreme. Phrases like "go with the flow" or "follow your instincts" are anathema to them. They're also not interested in intuitive approaches to problem-solving. For example, they would dismiss as totally ridiculous the idea that a health problem could be due to some sort of disharmony between the mind and the body, rather than a purely genetic or biological cause. And very few would think they could use visualization techniques to cure a serious illness such as cancer.

These people are at a point in their lives where they're generally pulling back from those experiences that get the blood rushing through one's veins. For many of them, such experiences never had any appeal in the first place. In a sense, they're out of touch with their own adrenaline, and that's the way they like it. The ecstasy that accompanies a moment of emotional intensity is now but a faded memory.

Women in this group express a strong sense of feeling disconnected from the world, a world that seems to have long ago forgotten them, or placed any value on the thousands of diapers changed, meals prepared, beds made. They're also quite fearful of the world — fearful of being unable to compete, fearful of the indignity of being ignored or feeling "invisible," and fearful of bodily violence. The men admit to none of these anxieties, but, on the other hand, enjoy no surfeit of self-confidence. In fact, like the women, they suffer from a sense of not being in control. To the men, the answer lies in a return to the "good old days" when you knew who was in charge. The women look to the government for security and to church and a visit from one of their children for comfort.

Extroverted Traditionalists

Approximately one-quarter of Canadians over the age of fifty can be classified as Extroverted Traditionalists. This group contains more women than men, and tends to be older and less affluent than average. Slightly higher than average proportions live in Quebec or the Maritimes. These people believe in "duty above all else," "family comes first," "a penny saved is a penny earned" and "Adam and Eve, not Adam and Steve."

We have called these 1.7 million Canadians Extroverted Traditionalists because they share many of the values held by the Rational Traditionalists, but their personalities evince a much more emotional, less rational approach to life. They are considerably more extroverted and socially involved. Their families are their number one priority in life, and they tend to be interested and active in all aspects of their communities, from the school board, to Neighbourhood Watch, to church bake sales. Extroverted Traditionalists are also very concerned with their personal status and the way in which they present themselves to the world. They really care what others think about them. For example, they choose their clothes and furnish their homes with great care and an eye to what others will find respectable.

Extroverted Traditionalists, more than any other segment of the population, have retained traditional religious beliefs and are actively involved in religious organizations. Their heavy participation in religious activities springs from both a strong quest for spiritual meaning and a pronounced need for community, both of which they find in church. In fact, they really do think of the place where they worship as *theirs*, in the sense that it is an integral component of the personal space in which they live their lives.

Members of this segment are very comfortable with the whole concept of a hierarchical, and even a hieratic (priest-ly) society. In their previous lives they might have fit very well into the Druid societies of early England or the fiefdom of a medieval European bishop. The deference that they give to authorities and institutions is not so much a sacri-fice of personal control as it is a source of solace, whether these authorities be religious, business or familial.

Extroverted Traditionalists believe strongly that young peo-ple should defer to the wisdom and direction of older peo-ple, in the way that they were taught to as youngsters, and in the way that they personally still defer to those in posi-tions of authority. Members of this tribe are almost unanimous in their belief that young people should be taught to obey, rather than question, authority, and that "good parents make and enforce strict rules for their children." And almost all would agree that young people today have "too much freedom and not enough discipline."

Extroverted Traditionalists believe strongly in an ordered existence. They don't like surprises or the general messiness that comes from allowing children to question their elders, or Sikhs to wear their turbans to the local Legion Hall. It is this need for order that, at least partly, inspires their preference for hierarchical structures. They feel much safer, for example, with organizations where orders come from the top down, rather than from the grass roots up.

At the same time, Extroverted Traditionalists cannot be dismissed as completely strait-laced. Quite the opposite: members of this segment tend to be highly emotional. They're motivated by sympathy and by love — of God, their family and community — and by fear. They are very unlikely to advocate any sort of social Darwinism, believing, correctly, that they would be among those most at risk were such an ideology to prevail. Beyond the obvious considerations of self-interest, support for Big Government among the members of this tribe is also dictated by their general predisposition to believe the best of those in authority.

Although they are the most god-fearing and law-abiding of Canadians, Extroverted Traditionalists have no illusions about others. They worry that they could easily fall victim to violence or other criminal activity, in their own communities or even in their own homes. These are people who are loath to walk outside alone after dark, and who keep their doors locked at all times.

Overall, Extroverted Traditionalists are an anxious lot, whether the issue is global or local. They believe that the coming millennium will bring major social upheavals and ecological catastrophes. They worry that new technologies will cause more problems than they solve. They worry about how they will manage financially during the years they have left on earth.

Interestingly, Extroverted Traditionalists are a somewhat paradoxical group. On the one hand, they tend to be quite fatalistic, in the sense that they believe much in life is beyond their control. However, they also express a greater than average confidence in their own inner resources, and in their ability to face life's complexities and challenges. These are not a bunch of cringing whiners. They take a great deal of pride in the fact that they have survived wars and economic depressions, not to mention more than a few personal crises. And they're still here!

Extroverted Traditionalists have mixed feelings about the explosion of new technologies that can either simplify or complicate their lives. As a result, their purchases of technological products tend to be utilitarian rather than experiential or aesthetic. They are more likely to own a microwave oven than a VCR or a CD player. And a person-al computer? "Let's discuss that after I figure out the auto-mated teller machine."

They are also very discriminating consumers who take the time, first, to decide if they really need a product, and if so, to seek out the best value for their money. Most of their purchasing behaviour tends to focus on considerations of usefulness. They prefer synthetic fabrics to cotton for their wrinkle-free utility. When Extroverted Traditionalists do make a purchase, they prefer that their possessions appear proper rather than striking or fashionable. Their status-seeking is based less on the desire for ostentation than on notions of propriety. They take the time to address small details of their appearance; for the men, the tie must be straight and the shoes polished; for the women, the hair must be coiffed and the bag must match the shoes. Miss Manners doesn't have a more devoted audience.

Extroverted Traditionalists are uncomfortable with the social changes that have taken place since the 1960s. Although most are not overtly racist, they do express a longing for the days when Canada was a more homoge-neous society. They firmly believe that immigrants of *different* racial and ethnic persuasions (i.e., non-British and non-European) should set aside their cultural backgrounds and try to blend into the so-called *Canadian* culture. Of course, this too is a form of racism, if much more polite than that of the Ku Klux Klan or the Aryan Nations.

In their personal lives, Extroverted Traditionalists are strong believers in marriage and fidelity and, despite the fact that most of them are women, reject the idea of women's absolute equality. In their opinion and experience, men and women *are* different. Therefore, it is only fitting that men fulfil certain traditional roles, while women fulfil others. Extroverted Traditionalists are even averse to androgynous styles of dress; not being able to tell the boys from the girls makes them very nervous.

They are horrified by what they see as an excessive preoccupation with sexual subjects in the mass media. And they are repulsed by alternative forms of family, such as common-law or same-sex relationships, judging them to be ungodly, unnatural or both. Many of them protested vociferously against protection for gays and lesbians in the Canadian Human Rights Act. *Their* morality is clear: obey the Ten Commandments and avoid the seven deadly sins.

Like the Rational Traditionalists, Extroverted Traditionalists have a strong sense of personal duty. However, in the case of the latter group, their sense of duty is at least partially fuelled by an equally strong fear of not being respected by others. Extroverted Traditionalists hope that, by being model members of organizations and model citizens, they will be given the recognition they feel they have earned. On the positive side, the combined motivations of fear and guilt make members of this group very useful — and sometimes irritating — people to have around. When they commit themselves to a job or a project, they give it their all.

On the negative side, this tends to make them highly judgmental of those who fail to live up to their standards, or who harbour values that diverge from their own.

But when it comes to duty to others, these people are at the head of the class. Some would even say they are generous to a fault with their children and grandchildren, with their friends, and with charities, especially religious ones. They are, in many cases, the financial backbone of what is left of the traditional religious establishment; they are also charitable toward the less fortunate in their own society and abroad.

Cosmopolitan Modernists

About one-fifth of Canadians over the age of fifty defy the societal stereotypes associated with old age. We have called these 1.4 million people Cosmopolitan Modernists. Whereas older Canadians tend to be sedentary, Cosmopolitan Modernists are nomadic. Whether or not they have travelled — and many of them have — they tend to look on life with a global perspective. A slightly higher than average proportion live in British Columbia. Like the other groups, certain catch-phrases capture their evolving mental posture. They started with "The world is my oyster," believed "progress is our most important product," thought and acted globally and locally, and now, later in life, are taking a little more time to "smell the roses."

This group skews toward a younger, more affluent and considerably better educated composition. Among older Canadians the pattern is clear: the more educated you are, the less traditional your values; this rule applies to a lesser extent among younger Canadians. Cosmopolitan Modernists obtained higher education when it was not as widely available as it is now, and, not surprisingly, many of them are professionals.

Members of this group are vigorous, self-confident and committed. They exude a strong sense of feeling in charge of their lives. They're the sort of people you see in commercials for low-fat cereals, kibitzing with their grown children, coaching their grandchild's hockey team, and planning an exotic vacation — all in a thirty-second spot. Partly because they tend to be among the younger pre-boomers, they are more likely than other older Canadians to be sexually active; the vast majority are married or in monogamous relationships. Most have fairly traditional marriages; he became a "master of the universe" as a professional in the world of business or public administration, while she assumed the role of wife, mother and chatelaine. Often one spouse played an instrumental role in the other's professional success. They express relatively little openness toward the idea of non-traditional relationships. For example, these are not people who would favour the legalization of gay marriages. However, even though they, themselves, have often embraced traditional roles, members of this segment offer strong support for the principle of equal rights for women. Both parents celebrate the success of the daughter who is now practising law or medicine, even if they remain a bit anxious about her finding a spouse and producing a grandchild.

On other questions, Cosmopolitan Modernists are less traditional and more modern than their age peers. However, it is a global perspective that most characterizes their world-view. They express a greater sense of being a part of the global village than do most Canadians. They are more likely than others to feel a connection with the world beyond our borders. For example, they are more likely to report regularly watching national and international news programs and documentaries. As a result, they are often better informed than the average Canadian.

It is this global consciousness among Cosmopolitan Modernists that drives much of their concern over ecological and environmental issues. They believe strongly that environmental protection must be a top public priority, even if it means having to sacrifice some jobs, and they are personally willing to pay higher prices for products that are more environmentally friendly.

It is from the tribe of Cosmopolitan Modernists that the current leaders in business and government are largely drawn. Whatever outside observers and critics might think, they see themselves as attempting, in the best way they know how, to "make sense of it all," and to find solutions to problems in a world in which the old rules have changed —or disappeared entirely. The difference between Cosmopolitan

Modernists and many of their age peers, such as the Rational Traditionalists, is the former's ability to embrace the complexities of modern life, and to see these as opportunities rather than as obstacles. The men, in particular, express a great deal of self-confidence in this respect.

More so than their age peers in the Traditionalist tribes, Cosmopolitan Modernists have found ways to have fun while doing their duty. These are people for whom spontaneity is an important part of everyday life. Often society's leaders, they get to travel and meet other interesting people, whether at work or play, or sitting on the board of some charitable organization. They love to eat in fine restaurants, drink varietal wines and debate the issues of the day.

Cosmopolitan Modernists tend to be very discriminating consumers. Because they're generally well informed, they know what's available in the marketplace and where they can find what they want, at the best price. No matter how affluent, or financially comfortable they are now, many of these people know what it's like to live without a great deal of disposable income. They're proud that they've moved up the financial ladder, and they consider their ability to manage their money an integral part of their personal success.

As I pointed out earlier, Cosmopolitan Modernists are not afraid of the challenges of everyday life. On the other hand, like most other seniors, they are often risk-averse, and have a strong sense of duty. Although they are among the least nationalistic of Canadians, they would be highly critical, for example, of someone cheating on his income tax, because they fundamentally believe in a system that has been very good to them. They are not averse to sharing "a piece of the pie" through government funding of social programs, because they believe we *all* benefit from Canada's social safety net, whether directly or indirectly. This is not to say they're not critical of current levels of taxation. However, their objections have more to do with what they perceive as mismanagement of resources than with a philosophical nod toward a social Darwinist style of governing. In addition, these people are often affluent enough that supporting social programs through higher taxes has little or no impact on their own lifestyles.

With some exceptions, Cosmopolitan Modernists, like the two Traditionalist segments, consider organized religion an important part of their lives. The women, especially, value the rituals that mark life's milestones. It is interesting to note that, although they generally harbour a modern and sociable world-view similar to that of the New Aquarian youth tribe, the issue of religion would divide these two groups into opposing camps: Cosmopolitan Modernists *for*, New Aquarians *against*.

4

THE BOOMERS:
BREAKING THE MOULD

"Canada is no longer a nation-state, but a postmodern
something."

— Richard Gwyn, *Nationalism without Walls*

We now turn our attention to a generation that, in many
ways, marked a radical break with the past. The years fol-
lowing World War II until the mid-1960s was a period of
exceptionally high natality rates in Canada and the United
States. The generation that emerged from this period is
known as the "baby boom." This was an era of unprecedented economic expansion, in which the meeting of basic
material needs could usually be taken for granted. This
affluence afforded large numbers of baby boomers who
grew up during this period the freedom to focus on self-fulfilment and idealism — from sexual freedom, to feminism
and civil rights. Television and rock 'n' roll helped to further
disseminate a culture of affluence, on the one hand, and of
social revolution, on the other.

The commonly accepted stereotype of the baby boomers is one of a somewhat spoiled, hedonistic, rebellious group. However, our analysis finds that this celebrated and controversial generation is divided among four tribes: the Autonomous Rebels, Anxious Communitarians, Connected Enthusiasts and Disengaged Darwinists. As the names of these tribes imply, the stereotype of the aging but still basically liberal, left-leaning, hedonistic "flower child" only scrapes the surface of the values profile of Canada's baby boomers. The picture is much more complex. In fact, only the first tribe is exceptionally rebellious, but their large numbers and the power of their message makes them the defining tribe of their generation.

Gail Sheehy, in *New Passages*,[5] makes the point that, in many ways, there has been a "ten-year shift" in life stages between the 1950s and the 1990s. "Adolescence" now goes on for far longer, even into one's late twenties. Every major life phase, from education, to marriage, to having kids, to death, has been pushed back a decade. As a result we're seeing an expansion of the earlier periods of the life cycle, and a compression of the later years. The one exception is employment, where, increasingly, retirement often takes place earlier, for example at age fifty-five rather than sixty-five, either because of personal choices made by employees, or down-sizing imposed by employers.

From the boomers' perspective, there is little reason to accept the traditional gender and life-cycle stereotypes. It's not just a matter of stretching out the average lifespan from fifty to eighty years, or of extending one or another of the stages within life. Rather, it is the confidence to discover and explore novel approaches to the sequencing of these stages, with the possibility of difference and repetition: having one child in your twenties and another in your forties; school in your teens and again in your fifties or seventies; childhood and adolescence (vacations) periodically throughout; work sporadically and as little as possible.

Let us now turn our attention to the four tribes that make up the baby-boom generation. I urge the reader to put aside the media stereotypes of the Woodstock generation and the movie *The Big Chill*. As is the case with the elders and Generation X, those stereotypes serve more to obfuscate than to illuminate our understanding of a generation whose influence on our own country, and on the world, has been profound.

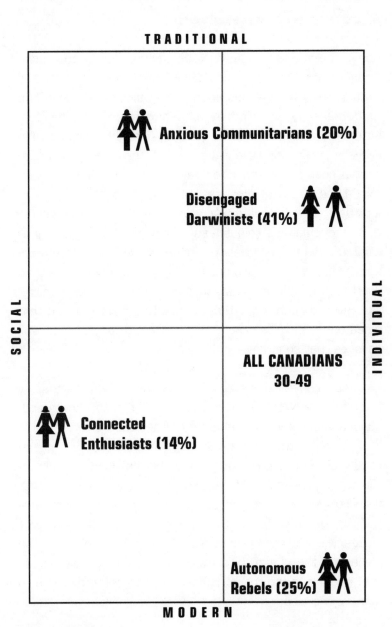

TRADITIONAL

Anxious Communitarians (20%)

Disengaged
Darwinists (41%)

SOCIAL

INDIVIDUAL

ALL CANADIANS
30-49

Connected
Enthusiasts (14%)

Autonomous
Rebels (25%)

MODERN

Environics

Autonomous Rebels

About one-quarter of the boomers fall into the Autonomous Rebels tribe. We have called these 2.4 million Canadians Autonomous Rebels, because their perspective on life is fundamentally oriented by a strong focus on individual autonomy and personal fulfilment. A slightly higher than average proportion lives in Vancouver. They are the quintes-sential boomers in that they have, to a large extent, main-tained the ideals of the late 1960s. Although only one of four boomer tribes, in many ways, they define their genera-tion in popular consciousness. They tend to have higher incomes and higher levels of education, and an above-aver-age proportion are professionals. They're the ones who used to say, "Never trust anybody over the age of thirty" and, even though today they themselves have crossed that milestone, there's a part of their collective psyche that still believes that aphorism.

Like me, many of these people were the first in their family to openly question, and then reject, religious authority and, subsequently, secular authorities. They were often the first in their family to go to university, where they were exposed to all sorts of tantalizing and "dangerous" ideas. Many of the women probably thought of themselves as "the first feminists since the suffragettes." And many were probably the first in their family to travel to exotic out-of-the-way places like Kathmandu or Costa Rica, and to go to these places on the cheap, hitchhiking and crashing with people they might see for only a night or two, before moving on to somewhere else.

Autonomous Rebels march to the beat of a different drum-
mer (and I don't necessarily mean Ringo Starr, although the
Beatles would certainly be among their important cultural
icons). Supertramp's "The Logical Song" expresses some of
the wistful idealism they continue to harbour. Even today
they feel the energy of the music (rock 'n' roll) that still
serves as the acoustic signature of their generation. For
them, the 1960s was a magical mystery tour in the exciting world of sex (before marriage), drugs (marijuana, hash
and LSD) and politics (civil disobedience to demand minority rights and protest the war in Vietnam). Autonomous
Rebels are quick to react to what they perceive as
hypocrisy, corruption, conspiracy and privilege, and to
assert what they feel is true, fair and authentic. Of course,
everyone takes great delight when a famous male member
of this boomer tribe is caught with his pants down, as in
the case of Bill Clinton, who also claims he "didn't inhale"
(marijuana). "Yeah, right" chimes the chorus.

If Pierre Trudeau is the icon for their Cosmopolitan
Modernist predecessors, the US president and his wife,
Hillary, are the ironic icons for the tribe of Autonomous
Rebels. Indigenous examples include deputy prime minister Sheila Copps, singer Neil Young and Robert Charlebois.
However, for these "rebels with many causes," it is almost
more instructive to look at the people they dismiss, dislike
and distrust. No one is higher on the list than "Tricky Dick,"
former US president Richard Nixon. A close second and
third on the list are once Senator Joseph McCarthy and FBI
Director J. Edgar Hoover — an unholy trinity who represent-

ed everything that these boomers hated most when they were young, and still despise today. Senator McCarthy may have been relegated to history's scrap heap by the time the boomers came of age, but the shadow of intolerance and hypocrisy that he cast still rallied the forces of rebellion in the 1960s. By the way, I have deliberately chosen several American examples because these boomers are among the Canadians who were most heavily influenced in their youth by American television, music and politics.

The most educated and affluent of boomers, Autonomous Rebels are notoriously suspicious of authority. In some ways, to understand their views of institutional authority, one has only to look to the TV show "The X-Files," or the films of Oliver Stone, a filmmaker whose work appears paranoid to some, and to others as a cry against the conspiracies of the past perpetuated by the "military-industrial complex" (in the oft-quoted phrase of US President Dwight Eisenhower). One of their favourite movies is Stanley Kubrick's *Dr. Strangelove* — the quintessential anti-war comedy.

This rejection of authority and scepticism regarding the motives of big business and big government is reflected in a strong concern for the environment, and an equally strong bent toward egalitarian ideals in the workplace and in society in general. Autonomous Rebels take a global view of environmental issues. They believe that real ecological balance is achievable, and are very concerned with what they see as an inadequate response on the part of the private and public sectors. They also believe strongly in the equality of women, ethnic minorities, young people and alternative family structures. They are people who express support, for instance, for employment equity legislation, and for family benefits for gay couples.

Many Autonomous Rebels have abandoned traditional religion, and instead embarked upon a spiritual quest that is far removed from the solace and guidance provided by established churches. To some extent, they still believe in "free love" and sexual permissiveness, despite concerns about AIDS, waning libidos, and the fact that many have entered committed relationships. They love the unexpected and the spontaneous, but within the context of retaining firm control over their lives.

This desire for control over one's personal life is sometimes at odds with the demands of the state, and most of the Vietnam draft dodgers who stayed here after President Carter's amnesty and who became "Canadians by choice," would be members of this tribe, the most famous of whom is science fiction/cyberpunk writer William Gibson. Autonomous Rebels reject what they would describe as "blind nationalism" and jingoistic talk of "duty to one's country." However, although they are strongly anti-authoritarian, they do not believe in a social Darwinistic, "every man for himself" approach to ordering society. Their support for the less fortunate is not motivated by fear of the consequences of inaction, or guilt over the historical oppression of minority groups, but rather by a firm belief in everyone's right to determine his or her own fate.

They are the ones having commitment and recommitment ceremonies (for both straight and gay couples), where the script is written by the celebrants, rather than by a priest, or rote quotations of sacred texts. They are also starting to express their values in the funeral services of their parents and, less frequently but sometimes more significantly, of their peers. Again, they are assuming more control over the ritual, bringing the values of individuality, authenticity, spontaneity and informality to ceremonies that in the traditional context often lacked these qualities.

Despite their relative affluence, Autonomous Rebels are experiential rather than material hedonists. Their lack of concern with traditional status symbols has its roots in their awareness of the symbolism attached to their political actions and consumer purchases. In their youth, many adopted a life of voluntary simplicity, living in modest student quarters and driving Volkswagen Beetles. Their rejection of conventional symbols of status led them to abandon American cars in the 1970s and 1980s for European and Japanese alternatives: Hondas and Saabs rather than Chevys and Buicks. Today, they still attach little or no importance to such conventional symbols of success as the monster home in the suburbs or the Cadillac in the driveway. They say they are more interested in a job that provides personal fulfilment than in a pay cheque with a lot of zeros (but this is easier to say when your pay cheque already has a lot of zeros).

Autonomous Rebels can be described as active rather than reactive. Very independent-minded, they are not easily seduced by the consumer economy. They express relatively little interest in what other people think of them, and except what they consider to be a healthy scepticism toward élites, try not to be too judgmental when it comes to others.

Members of this tribe express little need to connect emotionally with people outside their immediate circle of family and friends. Unlike the youth tribes who go on-line, Autonomous Rebels are not particularly interested in making new connections with people they've never met. Their motivation for being more "wired" than other boomers is the convenience, the information available and the sense of personal freedom that comes from cruising the information highway.

Nonetheless, Autonomous Rebels are interested, in an abstract way, in understanding how other people think, and they are open to others in the sense that they enjoy living in a multi-ethnic, pluralistic community. They don't feel the least bit threatened by the fact that they're living in a society that is in a state of constant flux. In fact, Autonomous Rebels are among the least fearful of Canadians, whether this concerns their physical safety or their financial future. This relative insouciance at the prospect of incessant change makes them the defining segment of their generation, and the vanguard of the turbulent era they have come to dominate.

Anxious Communitarians

Anxious Communitarians constitute about one-fifth of the baby-boom generation. As a group, these people are not very comfortable in the 1990s, a decade in which government support for the social safety net is threatened by dwindling public-sector resources, traditional institutions are under siege, and non-traditional relationships unbalance the orderly world that they have tried to create for themselves and their families. A group with average household incomes, this tribe has more women than men, and a slightly higher than average proportion lives in the Prairie provinces, or in small or mid-sized communities.

We have called these 2.1 million Canadians Anxious Communitarians, because their values are driven by a combination of anxiety and duty to others, whether their families or their communities. Their world-view is shaped by devotion to their communities and by the twin emotions of fear and guilt. They tend to be more sociable than other boomers, and are involved in what is happening in their local area. They really value warm, affectionate relationships with others, the kind of relationships in which grown children phone their mothers regularly, and people bother to send Christmas cards, birthday greetings and anniversary notes to everyone in their orbit: for them, the ideal world is a Hallmark commercial come to life. Cultural icons for the women might be Martha Stewart or Lynette Jennings.

Anxious Communitarians reject the sort of social Darwinism that characterizes much of the neo-conservative revolution of the 1990s. This rejection springs from their own financial vulnerability and from a genuine empathy with others. They believe that society has a responsibility to aid the less fortunate, a sense that is at least partially motivated by feelings of regret, or even guilt, that life is not a level playing field. They really worry, for instance, about street kids having no food or a place to sleep. On a more personal level, many Anxious Communitarians are burdened, albeit willingly, by responsibilities to children and to aging parents, and maybe even to siblings doing less well than themselves. In other words, these are people with broad shoulders, people who will take on the cares of others.

The very traditional values of Anxious Communitarians are anchored around the concepts of traditional religiosity and the importance of the family. They are less adaptable to complexity than are other Canadians, and, not surprisingly, are also less critical of authority. Their values are divided between the traditional and the modern. They believe in the equality of the sexes and of the races, but feel strongly that young people often do not know what is in their best interest, and therefore require the protection and direction of their elders.

Anxious Communitarians are among the most apocalyptic of Canadians. They fear that the world is in for major upheavals in the near future, whether religious, political, economic, social or ecological. They express a wide range of anxieties, from concern over violence, especially by youth, to fears they will not have enough money in their old age. The women, in particular, are intimidated by the explosion of new technologies in everyday life; where these innovations are concerned, they are much more likely to see the cloud than the silver lining. Anxious Communitarians exist in not-so-quiet desperation, often looking for simple solutions to complex problems. Politically, they account for at least part of the swing-vote mentality that resulted, for instance, in Ontario moving from a Liberal to a New Democratic to a Progressive Conservative government within the space of ten years.

Unlike many other boomers, Anxious Communitarians have not made the transition from status-seeking to experience-seeking values. They are highly conscious of their position in the pecking order, and the symbols of their relative status. However, they are not Type A individuals out to conquer the world. Their goals are more modest: what Anxious Communitarians desire is the respect of others. In the 1980s, they bought the suburban bungalow of their dreams, complete with the pool in the backyard and the Buick in the driveway. Now, in the downsized 1990s, they grasp these symbols like mountain-climbers clinging by their fingernails to the rocky edge of the cliff. Their status-seeking is not of a materialistic nature, nor do they seek to impress others by acquiring more symbols of success. They just want to keep what they have. More importantly, they want to be judged by what they *do for others*. They want recognition and a sense that their devotion and hard work are appreciated.

Connected Enthusiasts

About one-sixth of boomers fall into the Connected Enthusiasts tribe. A slightly higher than average proportion lives in the province of Quebec. As their name implies, this is the most sociable segment of boomers. In one way or another, members of this group build their lives around other people, whether it's doing things with and for other people or allowing their image of themselves to be defined by others. Members are not afraid to explore the worlds around and within. Connected Enthusiasts are also characterized by the intensity of their emotions and the essentially free rein given to the expression of these passions. Rationality plays a relatively minor role in their approach to life.

We have called these 1.4 million Canadians Connected Enthusiasts because their perspective on life revolves around a desire to interact with and understand others, both in their communities and in the world at large. They crave a sense of being "plugged in." They have strong attachments to the traditional communities of family, city and country, but are also very open to new types of communities and sexual diversity. The cozy group of academics in Denys Arcand's film *Decline of the American Empire* would find themselves in this tribe.

Despite the fact that they comprise the smallest tribe of boomers, Connected Enthusiasts are no less influential than the other tribes in determining popular culture; their impact derives from the fact that they are very tuned into the world around them, and highly capable and desirous of expressing themselves. The largely urban settings in which they find themselves also contributes to their influence in the marketplace of ideas and trends. When the trendy US coffee-plus franchise Starbucks expanded into Canada, Connected Enthusiasts were their first customers.

For better or for worse, Connected Enthusiasts are, in terms of their attitudes, the most youthful of boomers. They are much stronger than the rest of their generation on most of the experience-seeking trends. They want to squeeze everything they can out of this life, with little or no thought to the next. Enthusiastic explorers, they relish situations in which they can express their creativity and adaptability, and in which they can give full rein to their hedonistic bent — all values characteristic of youth. Connected Enthusiasts are ardent pursuers of the adrenaline rush that comes from taking risks. For people who are in their middle years, they are, in some ways, clinging to their youth; they are the Peter Pans of the boomer generation. Connected Enthusiasts do not feel in the least guilty for not "acting their age," and, in many respects, flout conventional age stereotypes through their attitudes and behaviour. They are acutely aware that their time on earth is limited, and want to compress as much as they can into the years that remain. To them, "age is a state of mind." They are unwilling to defer gratification until the "next life," or even until much later in this one. The Grass Roots song "Let's Live for Today" could be their anthem.

"Eat, drink and be merry, for tomorrow we may die!" The paradoxical nature of this bittersweet motto, which leavens the vibrancy of a natural *joie de vivre* with a sobering sense of fatalism, is a fair reflection of the somewhat schizophrenic values of Connected Enthusiasts. On the one hand, they embrace life and risk. On the other, they express a keen sense of their own mortality and, indeed, the vulnerability of the entire human species.

Connected Enthusiasts have a strong spiritual side, but it is one that seeks non-dogmatic, informal and often spontaneous avenues of expression. They are more likely to be found in the United Church, for example, than in fundamentalist sects that demand strict adherence to a rigid code of beliefs and behaviours. Their icon is Shirley MacLaine, ever searching for the latest venue and vehicle for spiritual renewal and everlasting youth. *The Celestine Prophesy* and *Sophie's World* figure prominently on their bookshelves. In Quebec, this spiritual quest has led to a prolific flowering of popular and high culture, as well as greater interest in New Age thought (the latter a trend shared by their peers in British Columbia's "Lotus Land").

Connected Enthusiasts are torn in their attitudes toward technology. Their enthusiasm about new technologies, and the possibilities these afford for interacting with others and exploring one's own self, is balanced by a marked awareness of, and concern for, the possible downside of technological developments (sometimes a reflection of some "bad trips" on the road of pharmacological experimentation).

Although Connected Enthusiasts express a fairly high level of anxiety regarding the economy, members of this tribe are gung-ho consumers. They are motivated by status and image considerations, as well as simply by the joy of consumption for its own sake. They love the wide variety of goods available to Canadians: like busy consumer bees, they help keep all those million-dollar malls and the latest specialty stores humming with activity. At the same time, Connected Enthusiasts take into account the ethics of the companies producing the goods they buy, and are willing to boycott individual preferred brands if they think that will protect the planet for future generations or advance the cause of human rights.

Members of this tribe are among the most ardent of aesthetes, attracted both to beautiful objects and beautiful people. They are prepared to go to great lengths to maintain or improve their physical appearance; their self-image is largely based on this, and they firmly believe they are worth the effort.

Connected Enthusiasts have embraced the hedonistic and generally egalitarian ideals of many of their fellow boomers. However, they are not rebels against the establishment and are not suspicious of authority. And though they harbour many of the values associated with youth, most Connected Enthusiasts do not regard young people as their equals. They may demand heterarchical structures for themselves, but see little reason to extend the same consideration to younger Canadians.

Disengaged Darwinists

The first three boomer tribes more or less conform to the stereotype of their generation, with the Autonomous Rebels defining the "pure" type. The final group, the Disengaged Darwinists, is not only the largest single segment of the boomer generation, but also the most different. In many ways, they are the antithesis of the 1960s social revolution.

About four in ten of Canada's baby boomers are Disengaged Darwinists. A slightly higher than average proportion lives in the Greater Toronto Area. This tribe is the usually "silent plurality" of boomers, and anyone wanting to understand the roots of the neo-conservative revolution of the 1990s must understand the mindset of these people. More than any of their peers, they belie the stereotypical image of the hedonistic, rebellious boomer. This group has more men than do other boomer tribes, and includes an above-average number of blue-collar workers. Many members of this tribe, by the mid-1980s, had worked their way up into the middle- or upper-middle- income brackets.

Because of their reticence, and lack of facility with new communication technologies, the views of the 4.3 million Disengaged Darwinists have not received the representation that a group that size would suggest (and, in their opinion, warrant). Those who have been shocked by the right-wing swing in Canada, especially in Ontario, either did not adequately take them into consideration or, because of their relative silence, underestimated their strength. When the Disengaged Darwinists join with the Rational Traditionalists, their counterparts among the older generation, they can be a powerful force, as was evident when the Reform Party burst onto the political scene in the 1993 federal election.

Members of this tribe tend to be younger boomers who, for a long time, watched silently and helplessly as their version of the Canadian dream disappeared. They have become social Darwinists because they feel no one, including governments, is looking out for their interests; therefore, it is up to each individual to "look out for Number One." Among the men in this group are a large number of what have come to be known as "angry white guys." Unlike many of their fellow boomers, they do not reject authority. As they see the world, it is often the "natural authority" of men like themselves that is under siege. Some of them are lower-level functionaries in the public and private sectors, who are resentful about their diminishing prospects. "My ancestors came here (from Britain or Europe) and opened up this country. I work hard and I deserve to have everything my father had, and more."

In addition to being angry, members of this tribe are just plain intimidated by change and the complexities of life. Their lack of confidence can be, at least partly, attributed to a strong sense of disconnectedness on a number of levels. For example, as the least "wired" boomers, they feel disengaged from the new technologies that have exploded into public consciousness during the course of this decade. As a result, they are anxious regarding their professional and financial futures, in a world in which the "wired" and the better educated increasingly have the upper hand.

Disengaged Darwinists believe that society has already changed too much, too quickly, and for the worse. This is particularly true since 1987 when the élite presented the country with Canada-US free trade and the Meech Lake constitutional accord. The former has, in their mind, caused grave economic uncertainty, and may even have resulted in what they believe is a more or less permanent state of recession, or even depression in the 1990s. And the Meech Lake accord, in their perspective completely unnecessary, led ultimately to the Charlottetown accord in 1992 — something they took great pleasure in defeating. From the perspective of a Disengaged Darwinist, constitutional proposals are a complete waste of time ("they do nothing for me"), and either give way too much, or way too little, to Quebec. Although many of these people survived the 1981-82 recession pretty well unscathed, the restructuring of the Canadian economy in the 1990s is taking its toll on these more vulnerable workers.

Like their Rational Traditionalist counterparts, they reject the direction their generational peers, the Autonomous Rebels, have led society. They do not support the idea of women's equality, or alternative family structures. They brand programs of affirmative action or employment equity for women or visible minorities as "reverse discrimination."

However, despite their desire, in some instances, to return to "the good old days," Disengaged Darwinists are not a traditional-values tribe; members have little attachment to religious institutions, spirituality, or religious dogma such as creationism. Moreover, despite their often heated "family-values" rhetoric, they are less attached than Canadians in general to family or community. They're too busy looking out for their own self-interest.

In a sense, God "died" for the Disengaged Darwinists some time ago. But, it is only in the past few years that the implications of this, notably the decline of guilt, have become manifest. In the past, they may have felt guilty about their anti-pluralistic (even bigoted) views, but in recent years they have been succoured by such events as the popular rejection of the Charlottetown constitutional accord, and the neo-conservative revolutions in Ontario and Alberta. In the past, when these people joined the older Traditionalists in opposing official bilingualism and multiculturalism, the metric system, the abolition of capital punishment, affirmative action and, more recently, gun-control legislation, they were dismissed as racists, reactionaries and Neanderthals, with only the tabloids and *The Western Report* to defend them. But now, the bankruptcy of the "old Canada" has robbed the liberal establishment of a lot of its moral authority — leaving room not just for Quebec nationalists, but also for anglo "reactionaries" to assert themselves.

Rather than feeling guilty themselves, Disengaged Darwinists are now attributing guilt to others. In their case, it is not so much the demise, but rather the redirection, of guilt. "It is not my fault that those on welfare barely have enough to subsist. It is their fault for lacking initiative or being unwilling to work," they may say, or, "It is not my fault I don't have a job; it is all that employment equity crap. And don't even get me started on multiculturalism or Canada's immigration policy!"

The sexism of Disengaged Darwinists is not due to any religious nostalgia or hankering for the days when "girls were girls," but rather, simple self-interest as they perceive it. Many men — and their wives — either do not understand affirmative action, or feel it leaves them with the short end of the stick. They have little interest in being able to put themselves in another's shoes, or to understand someone else's point of view. They lack the vitality that is associated with the desire to broaden one's experiences, or explore and develop various aspects of one's own personality. In their minds, they know what's right, and see no need to look any further.

Members of this tribe express little interest in experience-seeking, or even in fulfilment of higher ideals through work. As far as they're concerned, what's important is "the bottom line" and "putting bread on the table." Aesthetics, concern for the environment and human rights all take a back seat to utility and price when purchases are made. But they are not discriminating consumers. Disengaged Darwinists are simply uninterested in the "consumer experience"; they prefer to spend as little time as possible shopping.

sex in the snow

Status-seeking and image likewise mean little to them. The bumper sticker on the back of their 4x4 says "I'd rather be fishing"... preferably alone.

5

THE GEN XERS: HOTWIRED

"We rarely stray away from singing about anything other than what we know, which is school and girls ... None of us are really jaded, and we don't write songs about working in the fields and losing our jobs."
— Mike Clive, bass player for *The New Grand*

The past several years have seen much media attention focused on the generation that followed the boomers, popularly known as Generation X. Born between the mid-1960s and the early 1980s, this is the most complex of the generations, and by far the least understood in spite of its current celebrity.

Raised in an environment in which advanced technology, in the form of fax machines, cellular phones, VCRs and personal computers became ubiquitous, Generation X is, in many ways, the vanguard of multimedia. In Canada, it is the MuchMusic generation, people who have grown accustomed to an historically unprecedented barrage of media images and ideas. As a result, members of Generation X tend to be much more at ease than their elders with change and complexity, and with people who are different from themselves.

Our research indicates that there are a number of values that can be said to characterize this group in general. These include a penchant for experience-seeking, a confidence in their adaptability, and concern with their personal image among their peers. Contrary to popular wisdom, and unlike their parents and grandparents, members of this generation are not worried about the future. Our data indicate that they are social Darwinists who believe that life is a jungle in which only the strong survive, and that they are among the strong who will prevail.

More than any other generation in history, young Canadians have abandoned fear, guilt and duty as major motivating factors. Their elders probably find this hard to understand: in their minds, there are a lot of reasons why young people should feel fearful or guilty, but these sentiments have failed to take hold among the young themselves. Though overwhelmingly positive, there is a negative side to this fearlessness: many young people eschew condoms when having sex, smoke cigarettes with illusory impunity, or take enormous physical risks simply for the thrill of doing something dangerous and exciting. Bungee jumping is just the beginning.

Young Canadians eagerly embrace a number of egalitarian and pluralistic values, including flexible definitions of family, a permissive attitude regarding sex, a desire for egalitarian relationships with others, including their seniors, and the pursuit of happiness over devotion to duty. They reject traditional hierarchical relationships based on title, age, seniority or religious injunctions, and, in many cases, believe that traditional family, social and work relationships are, in large part, responsible for the political, economic and ecological problems that confront society in general, and their generation in particular. Overall, however, they express very little anxiety over these problems; they're much more focused on immediate gratification, whether experientially or in the consumption of material goods.

There has been some talk of a paradigm shift toward neo-conservatism among the young. However, our research finds that younger Canadians remain on the leading edge in the movement away from traditional values. In this respect, the spirit of 1968 is alive and well among today's youth. If anything, many Gen Xers are dismayed and angered by the neo-conservative shift in values among some baby boomers who formerly championed progressive ideals and practised what they preached.

As is the case with older generations, generalizations about Generation X tend to mask significant differences among young people. Our research shows that Canada's youth segment into five diverse tribes of individuals. It is these differences in values *within* Generation X that I will now discuss.

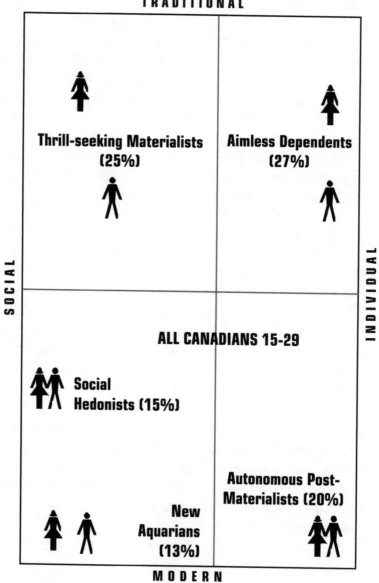

TRADITIONAL

Thrill-seeking Materialists
(25%)

Aimless Dependents
(27%)

SOCIAL

INDIVIDUAL

ALL CANADIANS 15-29

Social
Hedonists (15%)

Autonomous Post-
Materialists (20%)

New
Aquarians
(13%)

MODERN

Environics

Aimless Dependents

Aimless Dependents constitute just over a quarter of Canadians aged fifteen to twenty-nine. This 27 per cent of Canada's youth are the generational descendants of the Disengaged Darwinists among the baby boomers, and the Rational Traditionalists among the elders. The finding that they represent a smaller proportion of their generation than do their socio-cultural cognates is just one of several indicators illustrating the decline, in our culture, of a traditional and hyper-rational orientation to life, in favour of a more modern and experiential world-view (Disengaged Darwinists are 41 per cent of the boomers, and Rational Traditionalists are 54 per cent of the elders — twice the relative proportion represented by the Aimless Dependents).

The regional and demographic profile of Aimless Dependents mostly mirrors that of the general population. Although almost half have at least some post-secondary education, they are slightly less likely than other post-boomers to still be students, and more likely than average to be employed in pink- or blue-collar occupations. They are also slightly more likely than other post-boomers to be married, although over half are single.

Unlike youth in general, these 1.9 million young Canadians tend to approach life in a somewhat unemotional way, scoring low on values measuring an adventurous, open attitude to life. They don't believe in listening to their inner selves, and the idea of "going with one's gut" would be unsettling for them. Although they try to be *reasonable* rather than *emotional*, they sometimes explode, releasing pent-up anger and sexual frustration. This anger and frustration stems, in large part, from a very weak sense of being in control of their lives. The young men, in particular, have a strong sense of aimlessness and lack of meaning. Both men and women express relatively weak attachments to their families, their communities and to the world in general.

Sometimes characterized as "slackers," this tribe, more than any other, feels disconnected from society. The Aimless Dependents feel that everything has evolved too rapidly, often leaving them behind, like so much human detritus. They express little confidence in governments and in their own ability to navigate through the shoals of a rapidly changing world. This anxiety is expressed through an obsession with job security (as opposed to other employment considerations such as salary or the chance to be creative). Although their world-view is, in some ways, close to that of the Rational Traditionalists, Aimless Dependents have come to the conclusion that faith in society's institutions is ultimately untenable. Unfortunately, they have found nothing satisfactory to replace tradition, and as a result are "slackers without a cause."

Although not all Aimless Dependents take such a negative view of life, the most nihilistic of Canadian youth find a home in this tribe. Members are equally cold to organized religion and to inner spirituality, and to humanistic ideals such as equality of the sexes and of the races. The young men — lashing out at a world they feel neither cares for nor understands them — can be quite accepting of, and even prone to, violence. Moreover, this anger and resentment can be pathetically unfocused, leading to unprotected sex, teenage smoking, drug abuse, drinking and driving, quixotic violence or suicide. Its more anti-social aspect manifests itself in swarming, gay-bashing and mass vandalism of the kind sometimes sparked by major sports events, such as the Stanley Cup riots in Montreal in 1993 and in Vancouver in 1994, or conflagrations like the Yonge Street riot in Toronto in 1992 and the St. Jean Baptiste riot in Quebec City in 1996. Often the only mark they will leave on the world is through "tagging," applying their personal graffiti on public and private property. One of the most poignant examples of their pathetic nihilism was the 1995 story of three boys who travelled from Quebec to British Columbia, to emulate the suicide of their rock star hero, Kurt Cobain.

The young women who are Aimless Dependents tend to be fiscally conservative, for example, believing strongly in the value of saving money. Socially, their attitudes are a mixed bag: on the one hand, they're more open than many other Canadians to new definitions of family; on the other hand, they're only slightly more committed than their male counterparts — and much less committed than Canadians in general — to the principles of women's equality. In this tribe, neither men nor women could be described as egalitarian. When you look at the values of this tribe, at least two portraits emerge. On the one hand, you get a strong sense of people who have allowed their fears — and sometimes their laziness or inertia — to shut them off from much of what the world has to offer in terms of social, spiritual and material pleasures. The other picture that often emerges is that of people who are victims of circumstance. The protagonist of Jean-Claude Lauzon's film *Night Zoo* would find himself in this tribe, somewhat directionless after having left prison, and abused by the powers that be. "Des" from the CBC-TV movie *Little Criminals* would also be an Aimless Dependent, pathetically calm and solicitous around his alcoholic mother, and an explosive powder-keg around others. He would have been an Aimless Dependent — *had* he lived to the age of fifteen, instead of meeting a tragic and premature end.

Aimless Dependents are poor navigators in the consumer marketplace, and in life in general. The new technologies that promise so much are perceived by them as neither particularly exciting nor threatening. Members of this tribe report relatively low home-computer ownership levels and are the least likely of the youth tribes either to have an on-line service or even to use the computers that are in their homes. Many of the Aimless Dependents, unwired and unaware, think that the wonders of virtual reality are simply not salient to their existence. And when members of this tribe are asked about their sex lives, they emerge as a fairly monogamous group; few report having multiple partners (sometimes more the result of lack of success than lack of desire).

As might be expected, Aimless Dependents are quite parochial in their interests. They express little sense of being connected to what's happening in the world. For instance, only small proportions report regularly watching international newscasts or documentaries; they're much more likely to be tuned into a miniseries or TV movie, and they'd rather rent a movie and watch it at home on their VCR than go to the theatre for "the big-screen experience." In many ways, these are people seeking to escape from life, rather than live it to the fullest.

Thrill-seeking Materialists

About one-quarter of young Canadians can be classified as Thrill-seeking Materialists. A slightly higher than average proportion lives in Toronto. This is the "See and be seen" tribe. Somewhat younger than some other Gen Xers, many are fairly recently out of, or still in, school.

These 1.7 million young Canadians tend to be reactive rather than active. To them, who you are is less important than whom you know, how you look and what you own. They are the kind of people who like simple answers to questions or problems, so they can get on with enjoying life. For this reason their default position on issues is often the traditional one; the modern is too complex.

In many ways, Thrill-seeking Materialists are quite confident. Always looking for social cues from others, they are ready receptors for the myriad signals emerging from our consumer culture. What's cool? What's hot? What's happening? And they respond enthusiastically to all of these stimuli, wilfully or unconsciously playing the sedulous ape to their pop icons. Moreover, because Thrill-seeking Materialists are so open to the world around them, they also tend to be strong on a number of experiential trends. They're not averse to intense or novel experiences and the associated risks.

Overall, members of this tribe harbour an interesting mix of motivations, from the traditional ones of guilt and fear, to modern experience-seeking. However, a close examination reveals that this seemingly eclectic mix is in part the result of some differences between the men and the women. The young women, for example, are noticeably more anxious, both about economic matters and what they see as an explosion of violence in modern society. Both sexes are somewhat intimidated by new technologies; however, the young men are also excited by these new "toys," and the opportunity to show off the latest status symbols.

Unlike many other Generation Xers, Thrill-seeking Materialists express a strong attachment to and identification with Canada. But, their national pride is closely tied to a need to demonstrate its superiority over other nations. They also place a greater than average importance on a number of traditional symbols of national identity, including the flag, the national anthem, the Queen and the military. (It should be noted, however, that a majority of them dismiss the monarch as basically unimportant to the Canadian identity, an opinion that is shared by every single youth and boomer tribe.)   There may be interest in Buckingham Palace as the setting for a soap opera, but Prince Charles should not expect the kind of unquestioning allegiance older Canadian generations gave to his predecessors.

Thrill-seeking Materialists are among the most enthusiastic of Canadian shoppers. The young men, especially, are prime fodder for advertisers, expressing a lot of confidence in commercials. Both sexes are attracted by the aesthetics of advertising and by the cues it provides for what's new and trendy.   This week's designer label will be enthusiastically replaced by next week's, even more prominently displayed.

The objective is not to make the best buy, but rather, to make a purchase that will enhance their personal status. Thrill-seeking Materialists are ostentatious consumers, always wanting to prove to themselves and to the world that they are "winners" and part of the "in crowd."   Rather than define their own style, they react to what their friends are wearing and doing, and to images presented by the media.   It is extremely important to them that they fit in, and that they appear attractive to others.   "Beverly Hills, 90210" — that's the address they want.

It is this attitude that makes salary such an important job consideration for the men in this tribe.   After all, the zeros on their pay cheques are a universally and easily under-stood score card.   "Size isn't everything, except when it comes to salary." For Thrill-seeking Materialists, the only other employment consideration is job security. "A job with social meaning? Are you kidding? That's for wimps!"

On a number of social issues, Thrill-seeking Materialists are more conservative than their peers. In fact, within the context of their generation, they could be characterized as "New Traditionalists," even though they often lack the attachment to organized religion that brings comfort to their elders. Like people much older than themselves, they tend not to question traditional authority and the established way of doing things. And, like many of their elders, they are unconcerned about environmental issues.

The young men are quite reactionary when it comes to questions of equity and acceptance of people's differences, whether of an ethnic or sexual nature. They also believe quite strongly in a Darwinistic "every man for himself" approach to dealing with the inequalities that plague society. The young women, on the other hand, do support the basic principles of gender equality, perhaps because it is in their self-interest to do so. Both the young men and, somewhat surprisingly, the young women tend to accept violence, both as a thrilling component of entertainment on TV and in movies, and as a simple fact of real life.

Thrill-seeking Materialists express little interest in high culture such as live theatre or ballet. As might be expected, pop and rock is much more to their taste. They are also avid viewers of television. Living vicariously through documentaries, talk shows, sitcoms and music videos, their attraction to novelty is often motivated more by a desire to show others that they're connected, than by the desire to be better informed.

New Aquarians

A relatively small number of young Canadians, about one in eight, are members of the New Aquarians tribe. Their geographic distribution closely reflects that of the general population. They tend to be young, with a high proportion still teenagers. Generally more affluent than Aimless Dependents and Thrill-seeking Materialists, there is also, nonetheless, a larger than average contingent of New Aquarians in the lowest income category, perhaps because many are willing to accept a lower standard of living in order to leave home precociously and live according to their own rules.

We have labelled these 900,000 young Canadians New Aquarians because they have adopted many of the values associated with the much-heralded but yet unrealized "Age of Aquarius," including egalitarianism, ecologism, experience-seeking and hedonism. Moreover, they have repudiated values they see as conflicting with their world-view. Of all Canadians, New Aquarians are the most likely to have abandoned the traditional monotheistic religions of Judaism, Christianity and Islam. Part of their motivation for this is traditional patriarchal monotheism's misogyny and hostility toward gays. (Perhaps not surprisingly, the New Aquarians have a higher proportion of self-described gays, lesbians and bisexuals than any of the other eleven tribes.)

Of all the tribes, the New Aquarians are the most likely to describe themselves as having no religious affiliation, and to report that they never attend religious services of any kind. At the same time, they cannot be described as completely secular. They have given up on traditional religions, but are often drawn to other forms of spiritual exploration, for example the "New Age" of tarot cards, neo-paganism and astrology. The worship of Aphrodite may not be new, but it is certainly novel in the Canadian context. If the singer Tori Amos were Canadian, she'd be a New Aquarian. On a recent tour, her official concert T-shirts had the words "Recovering Christian" emblazoned on the front, and her album *Boys for Pele* was named for the Hawaiian goddess of destruction.

New Aquarians demand total control over their own lives, and believe that everyone should be accorded the same *right*; to them this is much more than a mere "privilege" granted at the discretion of some unreliable and untrustworthy authority. New Aquarians are strong believers in egalitarian values, and think it is up to the individual (rather than society or historical tradition) to decide his or her own social values and morals. They believe that young people should be treated as full members of society, with all of the attendant rights, and strongly believe in the equality of the sexes and the legitimacy of common-law and same-sex relationships. Their anti-authoritarian bent prompts them to question, and often reject, such institutions as governments and established religions.

New Aquarians are not very nationalistic. However, certain symbols of Canadian identity are significant for them: the natural environment, Canadian cultural products and the nation's multicultural heritage. Of notably less salience are such traditional and hierarchical symbols as the military, the governor-general and the monarch. Queen is a rock group, not some uptight English babe named Liz. As the most direct descendants of their Cosmopolitan Modernist and Autonomous Rebel predecessors, the New Aquarians are their generation's citizens of the global village.

Though strong proponents of individual rights, the New Aquarians' individualism is far from a hyper-egotism. On the contrary, the 3SC "synthesis" map of their values locates them in the experience-seeking "new communities" quadrant, the same quadrant where users of the Internet are found. Their world-view has an aggressive edge; they would agree with Nietzsche's observation that no creation is possible without some sort of destruction. They have broken with tradition, so as to create anew. Whereas the Aimless Dependents feel alienated because the world is changing too quickly, the New Aquarians often feel frustrated because things are too *slow* to change. They have seen their Autonomous Rebel baby-boomer predecessors, and upped the ante of progressive modernism. Together with their Autonomous Post-materialist cousins, they are the vanguard of post-modernity.

Not only are New Aquarians not afraid of taking risks, they tend to be among the most hedonistic of tribes, quite untouched by the twin emotions of guilt and fear. They express economic anxiety on some scales — they are more likely than their peers to consider themselves less well-off than their parents at the same age and to predict further deteriorations for future generations — but their penchant for risk-taking allows them to adopt a cavalier attitude toward their personal financial futures. At the same time, although they are among the more sexually active tribes, they are also more responsible than their peers in terms of adhering to the safe sex dictum of "no glove — no love."

New Aquarians are not particularly interested in what is happening in their local communities, in part because they are more likely than other Canadians to consider them-selves part of "virtual communities." They are the most "wired" of Canadians, with the highest rates of on-line ser-vice ownership, and their cybernomadic values are often a reflection of this. This is a group that is excited by the possibilities presented by new technologies, and whose enthusiasm is not dampened by concerns over the possible downside of technological progress. A New Aquarian can often be found in front of a PC rather than a TV, savouring the interactivity of the former over the passivity of the lat-ter.

New Aquarians are avid consumers of cultural products — movies and plays, concerts and dance — and of television sitcoms. Although they are sceptical of advertising, they enjoy its aesthetics. Their spending on leisure activities outweighs that of all other post-boomers, and the young women enjoy shopping, although for them it is not a matter of buying "what's in" so much as it is the rush of spending money on whatever big, or little, luxury item catches their eye. New Aquarians are not discriminating consumers, but are people for whom environmental considerations are important. They'd snap up a leather jacket, or a compact disc that caught their attention while they were watching MuchMusic, but carry their own mug to Starbucks to prevent another disposable cup from ending up in the local landfill.

New Aquarians are, in some respects, among the most post-modern of the youth tribes. They're the ones who are most open to the possibilities that life has to offer, whether that be surfing the Net or piloting a canoe through the penumbral mysteries of the Amazon. They are also the ones who are most capable of taking society in new and interesting directions, for the simple reason that they are not afraid to blaze new trails.

Autonomous Post-Materialists

About one-fifth of young Canadians belong to the Autonomous Post-Materialists segment. Their geographic distribution reflects that of the population in general. This tribe is one of the more affluent and, like the New Aquarians, tends to be composed of younger, single individuals. Autonomous Post-Materialists are the "natural children" of the Autonomous Rebels, in terms of values and world-view.

We have labelled these 1.4 million young Canadians Autonomous Post-Materialists because they are characterized by their strength on several values related to personal autonomy, and by their lack of interest in status considerations and material goods.

Like many other young people, members of this tribe reject the notions that deference should be paid to those in positions of authority, simply by virtue of their title, and that there are "proper ways to conduct oneself." However, Autonomous Post-Materialists have taken this rebellion to new heights. Moreover, their demands for personal autonomy include others who may also be in the position of having to defend their right to "a piece of the pie." Members of this tribe score high on egalitarian trends that measure support for equal rights for women and minorities. And they believe that young people can and should decide for themselves the conduct of their own lives. They brook no attempts at or pretensions of paternalism, no matter how well-intended.

Autonomous Post-Materialists have little attachment to the traditional nuclear family, and believe strongly in the legitimacy of alternative family structures. They may have grown up in the age of AIDS, but they are very much the "free love" proponents of the nineties, and perhaps of the millennium. In terms of sexual roles, the women of this tribe are quite open to exploring both the male and female sides of their personalities, while the men are secure in their own masculinity, though open to flexibility in others.

As might be expected among people who have rejected traditional notions of family and institutional authority, Autonomous Post-Materialists are among the least religious of all the tribes. Not only do they tend to dismiss the established churches as meaningless or even destructive in their lives, they express very little need for other avenues of spiritual discovery or comfort.

Among the men, the cult of individualism to which Autonomous Post-Materialists subscribe is accompanied by what might be conjectured as a surfeit of testosterone. This is reflected in a hard-edged social Darwinistic view of society that embraces risk and accepts the inevitability of an uneven playing field, and sometimes even of violence, as a natural part of life. Bart Simpson meets Xena, Warrior Princess. For their part, the women are noticeably unintimidated by the presence of violence in society; they don't accept violence as normative, but they're not about to give in to any anxieties they might have. When older women talk about "taking back the streets," these young women are on the front lines.

Though they enjoy having a good time, in some ways they are more serious, thoughtful and individualistic than others their age. For this reason, they are among the most difficult of Canadians to categorize, because they don't fit neatly into a stereotype. They will do their own thing, even risking public opprobrium, whether by agitating for a progressive but unpopular cause, or being the first on the block (in large cities) or in the community (most other places) to have a pierced nose, eyebrow or navel. And if they enjoy reading Hegel, or playing chess or the accordion, they'll do so — shamelessly!

As I mentioned earlier, Autonomous Post-Materialists are distinguished by their lack of concern for appearance or status. They show little concern for what other people think of them or how they are defined by others. Concepts like "keeping score" and "he who has the most toys wins" are meaningless. For them, style must give way to substance. Their hedonism is an active one of *doing*, rather than a reactive one of *having.* Many have recently left home, having made a conscious decision that personal freedom is more important than material possessions, at least for the time being.

Social Hedonists

A fairly small proportion of Canadians can be classified as Social Hedonists. Slightly higher than average proportions live in Ontario and Quebec. They are the "Don't worry, be happy" tribe. Members of this group tend to be younger, less affluent and less educated. More than any other segment of the population, the Social Hedonists are characterized by their focus on immediate gratification. They are among the most intense and, at the same time, the least analytical of Canadians. They subscribe to the French poet Paul Valéry's view that "there is nothing deeper than the skin."

We have labelled these 900,000 young Canadians Social Hedonists because they are primarily concerned with having a good time, with exploring the world around them, and with their image among their peers. In many ways they're quite confident of their ability to sail through life, albeit along a course set by others. They are creative and adaptable, and constantly in pursuit of the new, the exciting and the mysterious, living life for the moment.

They are the ones attending every concert and event for which they can get tickets, and eagerly and fearlessly braving the "mosh pit" where participants slam dance into each other, or "crowd surf," riding a wave of human hands. Often urban nomads, they roam the streets in large groups, looking for action. They have a limited attention span, and are easily bored when alone or without something to do.

Social Hedonists tend to be somewhat uncritical of the world around them. They express a fairly high degree of confidence in traditional institutions, including governments and business. Their intensity and hedonism are not connected to any sort of rebellion against the established order. In fact, they often take a positive view of the performance of the established order, and are more likely than their peers to think they are better off than their parents were at the same age, perhaps because they believe they are in an advanced, more intense psychic space.

As their name implies, Social Hedonists value the people in their lives. Their families and friends are important to them, and they're also very open to forming close relationships with a wide range of acquaintances, including people they might meet at rock concerts, all-night large-scale raves (events with recorded industrial, ambient and techno music), at other large public events or in their travels.

Social Hedonists are also aesthetes. They place a great deal of importance on how they look and on how other people look. It's also important to them that people recognize their achievements, although, as employees, they care a lot more about the bi-weekly cheque than other, less tangible rewards.

6

TECHNOLOGY: ETHNIC TRIBES AND CYBERNOMADS

"Scratch a Canadian and you'll get a theory of technology."
— Cybertheorist Arthur Kroker reflecting on
Canadians' historical preoccupation with technology

While I cannot offer the reader a complete theory of communications technology, I *will* provide some observations based on our socio-cultural research. All I ask you to remember is that these words of wisdom are from the same guy Marshall McLuhan rejected for membership in his Culture and Technology seminar in 1969. Earlier, Professor McLuhan's "the medium is the message" had vaulted him into international intellectual stardom. As a graduate student in sociology, I wished to join the Catholic priests, admen and other acolytes of Canada's most famous guru. After I had waited in line for an hour for an interview, the great man announced to me, as he relaxed in the lotus position in his little cottage at the University of Toronto: "I'm sorry, Mr. Adams, but sociologists can't think." So, dejected, I retreated to the Department of Sociology to resume my readings of Karl Marx, Max Weber and Talcott Parsons. Inspired by Professor McLuhan's words of encouragement, I became determined to co-found my own private research company, if only to put his aphorism to the test.

In his book, *The Skin of Culture*, McLuhanite Derrick de Kerckhove suggests that, from the moment they take to computers, children develop a kind of speed addiction, demanding that their favourite programs and games be immediately available. Certainly, it is a characteristic of children to be impatient and to demand immediate gratification of their desires. However, it is my belief that this description also characterizes a new Canadian mental posture.

Canadians are no longer willing to wait for gratification until death's door delivers them into an afterlife they're not even sure exists. And the camel-like sensibility that accepted the "burden" of whatever information was "pushed" upon it has been replaced by a childlike sensibility that will "pull" what it wants, when it wants it, and leave the rest behind. De Kerckhove concludes his book by predicting that "A new human is in the making." If my research is any indication, that new human may be a Canadian.

When our analysis of social values revealed that Canadians are divided into twelve values tribes, a question that immediately leapt to mind was "Why?" More specifically, why were younger Canadians, despite their fewer numbers, divided among more values tribes (five) than were boomers (four) or older Canadians (three)? The other, related question that presented itself was: why are demographic characteristics a more reliable predictor of tribal affiliation among older Canadians than among the young? Technology, I believe, provides part of the answer.

In the past, Canadians saw themselves in terms of "the three Rs" of race, religion and region. Today, religious tribalism plays only a marginal role in Canadian public life, and regionalism seems increasingly parochial and quaint in a world in which virtual presence is growing in importance, and Canadians in any region can communicate instantaneously, at little or no cost, with Canadians across the country and others around the world. The new communication technologies are now eroding the political and demographic borders separating Canadians from other people, and "de-territorializing" the country and the world. In the contemporary era, physical presence is becoming a less decisive factor in determining the community — or communities — to which one belongs.

And despite the presence of ethnic tribalism in Quebec, time is on the side of a more cosmopolitan, post-modern world-view on the part of all Canadians, including Quebecers. The ethnic communitarianism to which separatism appeals is as much an appeal to the past as it is to the future of greater personal autonomy, new connections and multiple identities.

sex in the snow

In Canada, "sex, drugs and rock 'n' roll" has given way to
"sex, *tech* and rock 'n' roll." In the same way that ecologism can provide a sense of the interconnectedness of
nature, new communications technologies, especially the
Internet, are providing Canadians with an exciting new
sense of social connectedness. Despite the misgivings of
some critics that the new technology is dissolving attachments to traditional forms of community, such as the family, church and state, there has actually been a *broadening*
of the definition of community to include new relationships
and new possibilities for contact that were formerly impossible, or prohibitively difficult, to establish. In the past, you
had it made in Canada if they let you join the club. Today,
you have it made if you can network in cyberspace.

As large, traditional and hierarchical institutions become
less relevant to Canadians, new forms of social organization — less formal and less structured — become possible, and even necessary. Rigid bureaucratic systems are
replaced by flexible, task-oriented projects, with everyone
on the team plugged in via personal computer, e-mail and
the Internet. Just as television transformed the worlds of
leisure and politics a generation ago, so too the personal
computer has revolutionized the world of work in the
1990s.

In addition to providing opportunities for new communities
and connections with other people, new interactive information technology allows Canadians to explore and express
different facets of their own personalities, unburdened by

Canadians Who Have On-Line
Services (Internet, CompuServe, etc.)
3SC Canada

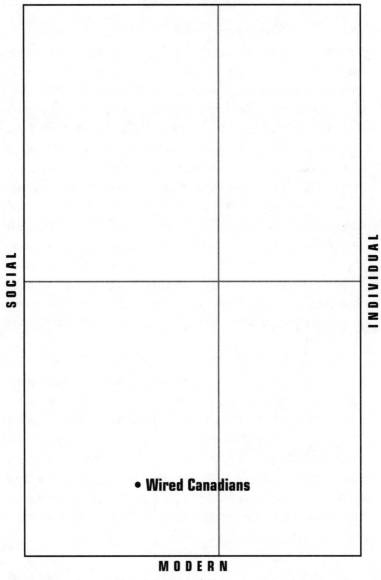

TRADITIONAL

SOCIAL

INDIVIDUAL

• Wired Canadians

MODERN

Environics

such demographic characteristics as sex, race or region. It allows for the personality equivalent of digital compression.

This idea of multiple-personality compression occurred to me one day when studying the lower-left "experience-seeking" quadrant of the socio-cultural map. It is apparent from the values important to people in this quadrant — flexibility of personality and gender identity, vitality, intuitive potential, interest in the mysterious, adaptability to complexity — that these people savour the prospect of new mental and emotional frontiers. And in fact, wired Canadians find themselves in this quadrant. When you combine these new mental postures with their enthusiasm for technology, it is easy to see how they wish to use the new interactive technologies to invent and reinvent themselves, and to connect with others around the world who wish to do the same. Thanks to the Internet, the complexity of the socio-cultural macrocosm can be reflected in the microcosm of the individual, and vice versa. The global personality in the global village.

Historically, in Canada, a relatively small population scattered in pockets across a massive geographic area necessitated a focus on means of physical transportation and communication infrastructure. In the current post-industrial era, the harvesting of material resources is accompanied — and often eclipsed — by a new focus on intellectual resources. Bits and bytes are becoming as important, or more important, than atoms, and "virtual transportation," or the communication of information, has become as critical as more traditional means of transportation. It is becoming as integral a part of the Canadian psyche in the 1990s as John A.'s "ribbon of steel" was a century ago.

Statistics Canada has reported that, during the period 1981–1994, computers enjoyed the largest annual growth rate in real spending of all consumer products examined, an impressive 20 per cent annually. As a point of comparison, during the same period, spending on audio-visual electronics climbed at an average rate of 9 per cent annually, and real spending on such products as new cars, movies, tobacco and alcohol declined.

Given this perspective, it is not surprising that Canada has given rise to world-class telecommunications companies, and is, in many ways, on the leading edge of technology adoption. Indeed, a *Times Mirror* survey, in which my company participated in 1994, found that, among the countries of North America and Europe, Canada has the highest level of home PC use. Canadians are also among the most wired people in the world; a 1996 international survey conducted by the IRIS network of research companies, including Environics in Canada, found that Canadians and Americans lead the pack in the rate of Internet access at home. Despite the challenge of keeping up with the most powerful economy in the world, on numerous registers regarding the popular adoption of technology, Canadians equal or surpass Americans. In May 1995, 340 new Internet domains were registered in Manhattan; 343 new domains were registered in far less populous British

Columbia. And on the music charts, Canadian singer Sarah McLachlan's CD-ROM disc, *The Freedom Sessions*, had the distinction of having been the first CD-ROM disc ever to place on the *Billboard* Top 200 albums chart.[6]

Bill Gates, Chairman and CEO of Microsoft Corporation, has suggested that the high level of cable penetration in Canada affords us a competitive advantage over all other countries of the world, including the United States, in the establishment of new telecommunications offerings. Japan, normally a leader in the development and embrace of new technology, has, for reasons of language and culture, been relatively slow in embracing e-mail and the heterarchical Internet. On the other hand, Canadians' growing rejection of authority, and demand for immediate gratification, is a favourable cultural — or counter-cultural — environment for the flourishing of new information technologies.

In Canada, personal choice is increasingly replacing mass culture, and this trend is being facilitated by advances in technology. When there was little or no choice on television, the medium served as a force of social homogenization and conformity. Canadians, from coast to coast, received the same messages and the same editorial points of view: a dominant culture was "pushed" at the viewer. At the same time, television was moving Canadians toward a new kind of emotional connection with people all around the world. Though limited in its perspective, the television camera forced people to become more cosmopolitan. With the introduction of cable TV, pay TV, satellite TV,

VCRs and the Internet, Canadians are now able to watch what they want, when they want. They are able to "pull" what they want from a wide range of media. The result is more individualized and idiosyncratic world-views, and the ability to become more cosmopolitan — or less — as desire dictates.

Today, Canadians are exposed to a myriad of different messages from sources that often contradict one another. This has contributed to the emergence of a population that is more suspicious and critical of what it hears, with both the positive and negative results that can be expected from that development. In their search for everlasting life on this planet, many Canadians have moved from "blind" faith in doctors and other medical professionals, and reliance on technology — drugs, lasers and CAT scanners — to autonomous self-regulation — diet, exercise, cessation of harmful habits like smoking and unprotected sex — to new age and oriental approaches — acupuncture, herbal medicines, meditation and even crystals. In a world where anything goes, there is much that is positive, particularly in terms of widening choice and individual control. However, there is also the potential for abuse and exploitation by not always well motivated "quacks" willing to exploit the ingenuous, the vulnerable and the desperate.

Today if wired Canadians detect strange symptoms, they can see their doctor *and* consult the Net, then take the advice of both. Being God can sometimes be an awesome, even frightening, responsibility as you move along the spectrum from consumer choices at the Sears store to matters of life and death.

A breakdown in consensus over social values has also resulted in a culture that has few illusions about its uniformity. In the past, most Canadians had a fairly well defined stereotype of what constituted a "Canadian." Now we have to ask ourselves, "Which one?" or "Which tribe?" "A typical Albertan? Is that Preston Manning or k.d. lang?"

Often the gaps in understanding are generational. A friend of mine recounted that he used to watch Johnny Carson's monologues on the "Tonight Show" and get all the jokes, as did his parents. Recently, he listened to a David Letterman "top ten" list without recognizing a single name, while the studio audience, mostly people in their twenties and thirties, howled with approval. My friend's parents haven't even heard of David Letterman.

This is just one example illustrating the point that television is losing its power as a force of social homogenization and integration. The 3.5 billion audience for the Olympics is the exception, not the rule. As I mentioned earlier, this can be partly attributed to the popularization of alternative uses of the medium, such as watching videos or playing video games. It can also be partly blamed on the more general cultural phenomenon of declining confidence in institutions. The proportion of Canadians who strongly agree that television plays a very important role in their daily lives has declined significantly during the past decade, from 27 per cent in 1986 to 17 per cent in 1995.[7] Though Canadians continue to watch a lot of television — on average twenty-two to twenty-three hours per week — viewership has been basically flat in Canada for the past decade. But, older Canadians have been watching the same amount or more than previously, and the more modern youth tribes have been watching the same amount or less. On average, those over the age of sixty watch about thirty hours of television per week, while teenagers watch under twenty hours per week.[8] This phenomenon partially explains the greater social fragmentation among the young. Undoubtedly this trend will grow as a nation of viewers, empowered and enthralled by their ability to develop their own highly per-sonalized world-views and find their own tribes, increasingly utilize alternative sources of information and entertainment, particularly on-line services.

In the same way that affluence led — or at least allowed — boomers to question the values of their parents, advanced communication technologies are exposing young Canadians to a wide spectrum of values, and affording them the opportunity to question the values of their own parents, the baby boomers. Many young Canadians have adopted the values of their parents. But, like the boomers before them, many others, like the New Aquarians profiled in the previ-ous chapter, have created their own unique sets of values.

If we want to talk about two solitudes in Canada, we could plausibly talk about the gulf separating the young from the old as being far greater than that separating Quebecers from other Canadians. It is among the young that social consensus is most centrifugal, as illustrated by the five values tribes of youth revealed by our segmentation analysis of Canadian values.

It is not surprising, then, that some critics have attacked the information explosion, and the Internet in particular, as subversive, pornographic, a waste of time due to a surfeit of unanalyzed information, or all of these. Clifford Stoll, author of *Silicon Snake Oil*,[9] attacks not so much computers as computer culture. He worries that for some people, living on-line has replaced living in the physical world. Cultural critic Mark Slouka makes a similar point, warning of the danger of representations of reality (virtual reality or VR) becoming more important in some people's minds than the real thing (real life or RL).[10] Others point to an avalanche of unmediated and unedited information.

Although a flood of unanalyzed data *does* mean more work for those receiving the information, it also means that their choices or interpretations are not mediated by a moralizing élite or the censorship of public opinion. In addition, the above-mentioned criticisms beg the rejoinder that, whether critics like it or not, virtual reality is now a significant dimension of everyday reality, and whether or not they choose to participate or approve is of little concern to those who do.

In fact, Canadians' growing rejection of their institutional élites is reflected in their enthusiasm for on-line experiences and networking. This includes reading, writing and viewing what they wish, without the interference of the police, customs agents or, for that matter, their parents. In an environment no longer ruled by religion or the state, the disposition of our time and discretionary dollars will be truly voluntary, extracted neither by guilt, nor the imposition of law, nor fear of social sanction. The medium is the Net, and the motives are experience-seeking, a quest for meaning, and (Net)working to create communities of interest and engage in mutually beneficial projects and emotionally fulfilling relationships.

As *Wired* magazine guru Nicholas Negroponte, among others, has pointed out, in the area of marketing, the popularization of the Internet has given a breath of new life to small business. In his view, companies can now be both small and global at the same time. Through thoughtful niche marketing, small businesses can achieve great success, at modest expense, by catering to increasingly specific international markets. One can benefit from the simultaneous growth of interconnectedness, social fragmentation, and the demand for immediate gratification by appealing to more personalized tastes around the world.

These include more personalized tastes of a sexual nature. Erotica, of course, is now more available than ever, from the corner store to the video outlet. However, pornography on the Internet has provoked a particularly heated response. In 1993, researchers at Carnegie Mellon University prepared a controversial study entitled

sex in the snow

Marketing Pornography on the Information Superhighway.[11]
This study concluded that on-line porn is very popular, and
that images of various perversions are not difficult to find
on the Internet. However, it also found that pornographic-
image files comprise only a tiny proportion of all the messages on the Usenet newsgroups, and that the Usenet
itself is only a small part of the traffic on the Internet.

Though there are programs such as NetNanny or
SurfWatch to protect children or adults from prurient
images on the Net, calls for, and attempts at, censorship
continue to mount. Though, in my view, there are genuine
concerns, the intensity of calls to censor the Internet
springs from more than simply distaste for the images presented. As is often the case, the issues raised by critics
are sex (for example, pornography), violence (for example,
the paranoid rants of some neo-Nazis) and paternalism
(the corrupting of our youth).

Part of the conflict centres around the fact that those most
in favour of such censorship — the Traditionalist segments
at the top of our socio-cultural map — are not the same
people who are using the Internet — the Autonomous
Rebel boomers and the youth tribes, especially the New
Aquarians right at the bottom of the map. There is also
the nature of the medium. Cyberporn can be obtained at
low cost, and without having to deal with the guilt or dis-
comfort some feel walking into a porn shop. And you can
experiment with different types of materials, downloading
only images in which you are interested, rather than having

to purchase a magazine or video, most of which does not appeal to you. It is perhaps not surprising that the tribe with the highest proportion of self-identified gays and lesbians, the New Aquarians, is also the most wired.

Of course, we have visited this territory before with each new medium, whether print, movies, live theatre, magazines, comic books, radio, television, music or the visual arts. Each of these media has at one time or another violated community standards of decency, thereby eliciting outrage and efforts to censor. Examples are legion, although the decline of traditional values and the rise of autonomy and hedonism have both diminished the intensity of public reaction and the basis of public concern. From a violation of our Judeo-Christian code of ethics, the debate has shifted to the possible anti-social consequences of exposure to violent and exotic stimuli, which in turn has meant that the subject of concern has often shifted from sex to violence.

Social scientists have been studying the effects of media exposure to sexually explicit and violent content for decades. They have found that children exposed to the Three Stooges or the Power Rangers are more likely to prick balloons than those who watch Barney the dinosaur or Sesame Street. But, so far, they have been unable to correlate exposure to Hamlet or King Lear to the incidence of regicide.

In the end, both those who wish to censor and those who

feel just as strongly about freedom of speech and expression are coming to recognize that media content is becoming much more difficult, if not impossible, to regulate. Like the weather, we take what comes, and deal as best we can with the consequences.

Cosmopolitan Modernists, the most advanced tribe among older Canadians, are far more wired than their Rational and Extroverted Traditionalist counterparts. However, even this segment is less wired than the youth tribes. While nomadic Cosmopolitan Modernists are actually hopping trains, boats and planes, their young counterparts, the New Aquarians, are cybernomadic and are travelling *virtually*. This is one reason it can be expected that New Aquarians will be more successful than any of the older tribes in exporting their world-view to their own, previous and subsequent generations.

Although, so far, women are under-represented among those on-line, there are good reasons to believe this situation will change. The progressive and non-misogynistic attitudes of those currently on-line, especially evident among the New Aquarians, suggest a warm welcome to women's greater participation. So too does the more obvious motivation to emotionally connect virtually, and possibly in person. Although cybernomads are currently relatively few, they tend to be progressive in their values (located in the lower-left experience-seeking new-communities quadrant), and enthusiastic in their proselytizing on the virtues of becoming wired. As computers develop a greater presence in formal education, from pre-schools to universities, women, who are already well-represented in these institutions, will achieve more equal representation on-line. Many post-secondary institutions now arrange an Internet account for each student as a standard service; undoubtedly this will also encourage greater participation by women.

Apple Computer commissioned Rosalind Resnick, editor of *Interactive Publishing Alert*, to undertake a survey of women on-line, to determine why women are under-represented, and what can be done to address this.[12] Some women said they were offended by sexist remarks and "flames" (insults in cyberspace), and would prefer greater censorship of such material. However, the main factors preventing women from participating more on-line were a lack of time and money — pretty universal concerns, and ones that still hold today.

In spite of the current gender gap, our research finds that the main differences in motivations for going on-line are not between men and women, but between the generations. Younger Canadians are more attracted to the experience-seeking, exploring and communicating with friends and strangers, whereas older Canadians (mainly boomers) are more attracted by the time-saving convenience and the informational content of the Net.

Even if women catch up to men on-line, the medium is still far from representative of the population as a whole. The popularization of these technologies dissolves some borders, and the *de jure* barriers (such as state and provincial boundaries) are diminishing in significance. However, at the same time, other *de facto* divisions, such as the urban-rural divide, are emerging into stark relief. The adoption of technology in Canada is slanted toward younger rather than older users, urban rather than rural users, and toward the better educated and more affluent.

Although the Internet is not yet fully democratic, some critics have attacked what democratization there is. They preferred the good old days when the *hoi polloi* weren't able to participate in discussions previously limited to professional and academic élites. However, with the doors to post-secondary education becoming more difficult to enter for increasing numbers of Canadians, it is serendipitous — and perhaps *not* coincidental — that young Canadians are embracing these technologies with such enthusiasm.

With tuition fees at universities and community colleges rising steeply year after year, the traditional route of social mobility, post-secondary education, is becoming less accessible to some. In fact, recent years have witnessed the first declines in decades in applications for enrolment in these institutions. In this context, the wide dissemination of personal computers and access to on-line services becomes all the more important. Increasingly, personal empowerment begins with a personal computer. So though the most recent middle-class ambition of "a house, a car and a VCR" may be within reach for many Canadians, it would probably be wise to purchase a personal computer and an on-line service if you hope to someday own the others.

In the cybernomadic tribe, your sex, race, region and age matter less than your ability to convey your message clearly and compellingly, for the simple reason that these demographic characteristics are not immediately apparent. Canadian youth, although disadvantaged at the ballot box, might reasonably expect a greater degree of fairness and success on-line than in many other arenas of life.

If my reading of social trends is correct, the Net will prove to be the medium of choice in the early days of the next century for North Americans who wish to find new pastures for intellectual, emotional and sexual intimacy. The exercise of personal choice, the temporal and serial nature of relationships, the quest for meaning and sensual pleasure — all indicate a huge potential demand for introducing kindred bodies and spirits. The services will range from standard heterosexual dating to XXX-rated S&M and beyond. The possibilities are limitless, which means we are entering the exciting — and frightening — world of "pulp non-fiction."

7

WOMEN AND MEN: FROM TWO SOLITUDES TO FLEXIBLE IDENTITIES

"I find people in general sexually attractive. But then I find trees sexually attractive, too."

— Singer Sarah McLachlan,
when asked whether she was straight or lesbian

An aspiring sociologist once said, "There are basically two types of people on this planet: men and women." In my experience as a researcher — and as someone who has tried to feel personal empathy for the women I have known — I have found that there are broad generalized differences in the ways that women and men view the world around them, and in the ways that they relate and communicate with the people in their lives. However, my research has shown me that the differences in values between men and women are not as great as is often supposed, and certainly not as great as what up till recently was dictated by tradition. Further, the seminal differences pale in comparison to those among the values tribes. Believe it or not, Canadian

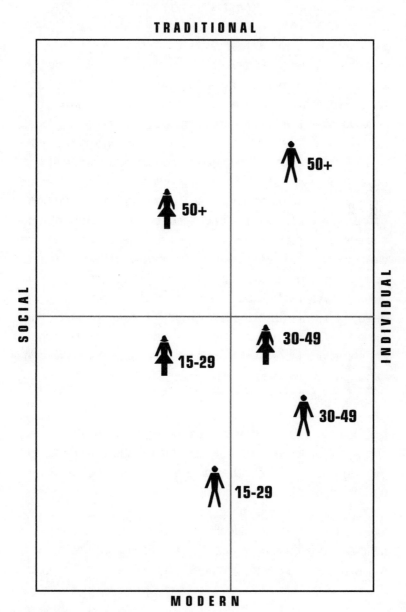

Environics

women and men are from the same planet!

Until very recently, women were too often treated as sec-
ond-class citizens. Today, on paper at least, they enjoy the
same rights as men. They sometimes have to fight harder
than men to make this equality a reality in their lives, but
they do have the weight of recent political force and legal
precedent in their favour. And however much more needs
to be done, certainly this gives today's women a distinct
advantage over their Canadian predecessors and over
women in most other countries of the world. In addition,
some women, at least, have profited from the radical
change in social values toward the role and status of
women, as well as implementation of affirmative
action/employment equity programs in hiring and promotion
policies. As is often the case among those who might be
described as "historically myopic," the success of the
movement to correct centuries of discrimination by applying some pressure in the opposite direction has created a
backlash: among some, women are seen as having some
sort of "equal status plus."

My focus in this book, of course, is not on what should be,
but what is. I therefore will not debate the civil rights of
men and women, but rather discuss the nature of their values and how these have changed dramatically in what is a
nanosecond when measured against the millennia of historical tradition since the Neolithic revolution. Nonetheless, I
believe this particular legacy of the 1960s social revolution
will prove to be most profound and enduring. For both

"boys and girls," the rules have changed, and the traditional balance of power has shifted forever.

In a nutshell, our social-values research shows that the value profiles of men and women still differ in many respects. However, age and occupation, for example, are much better predictors of values than is gender. Working women share more values with working men than they do with housewives, and young women share more values with young men than with older women, as author Kate Fillion, among others, has recently pointed out.[13]

It wasn't very long ago that it was possible to sum up the motivation of women in two words: "guilt" and "duty." Women lived lives of self-sacrifice for others: parents, spouse and children. When we buried them, we called them "saints." Today, however, the values propelling our culture — autonomy, hedonism and a quest for meaning — have influenced women as much as men. Former pop star Cindy Lauper may have overstated it somewhat when she declared "Girls Just Want to Have Fun," but the days of "Queen for a Day" — the 1950s quiz show that crowned as queen the woman with the most pathetic hard-luck story — are over.

I predict that there will always be differences between the social values of men and women, but that these differences will diminish over time. Moreover, the differences will become less predictable, as the stereotypes that define men and women become even more muted than they are today. However, the differences that remain will still be quite significant, leaving lots of room for the many factors that attract the sexes to each other, and occasionally repel them from each other.

In earlier days of feminism, it became customary for women to dress like men — thus pants and shoulder pads, and even eschewing the bra. Today, when by all measures women are more equal to men, it is possible to be feminist and feminine, and women's choice of clothes is more eclectic — sometimes formal, sometimes informal; sometimes the unisex jeans, sometimes the feminine dress; sometimes modest and sometimes a sexy, revealing *décolletage*. Sex and/or snow, depending on one's mood, attitude or intent.

The primary area in which there remain dramatic differences between the values of men and women is in their orientation toward violence. Men are significantly more likely than women to believe that violence is an unavoidable fact of everyday life, and an acceptable way of resolving disputes; men are also much more likely than women to be entertained by violent sports, movies or television. Women, on the other hand, are much less likely to accept violence as normative, and much more likely to worry about being violently attacked or victimized.

There are important generational differences in the trends measuring acceptance of violence as normative and fear that one will be a victim of violence. In the area of acceptance

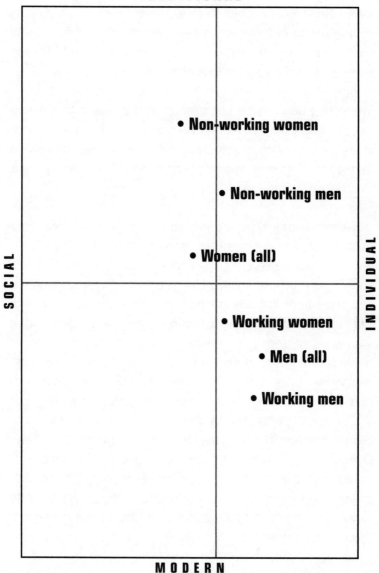

TRADITIONAL

SOCIAL

INDIVIDUAL

• Non-working women

• Non-working men

• Women (all)

• Working women

• Men (all)

• Working men

MODERN

Environics

of violence, all the Generation X tribes score higher than average; among all the older tribes, only Disengaged Darwinists score higher than average. There is much less of a generational pattern regarding fear of violence: some youth tribes score *higher* than average on this trend, and some older tribes score *lower* than average.

There has been much speculation in the media that young people, and young women in particular, are becoming more violent. This phenomenon was reflected in the emergence this decade of new aggressive girl bands, known as "Riot Grrls" ("grr" as in "growl").

Although these bands represent a somewhat extreme expression, these kinds of aggressive attitudes are probably much more prevalent than some would like to admit. Of course, there have always been openly aggressive women, but they had virtually no acceptance, nor any icons, in mainstream culture (with the possible exception of Mae West). But today, these bands are an integral part of mainstream youth culture. I realize this is not very reassuring for those who believe that the "Riot Grrl" phenomenon is contributing to an aggressive attitude among the young women who look to these performers as role models. Commenting on the 1996 Fête Nationale riot in Quebec City, Jean-Yves Légaré, a constable responsible for protecting the national assembly remarked, "What surprised me was the number of women. They were tossing rocks with the others." Riot grrls, literally, perpetuating violence in the snow.

Certainly, the past few years have seen a couple of high-profile cases in which young women have apparently committed crimes often thought "unthinkable" for women. Canadians listened with horror to the story of Karla Homolka's role in the sexual torture and murder of two young girls, as well as the rape of her younger sister and another unnamed victim. In July 1995, Calgary police charged three teenage girls with robbery and manslaughter in the fatal stabbing of a man who had stopped his car to help them.

In the Homolka case, much of the controversy centred around the issue of whether Karla was coerced into a life of crime as a result of abuse by her husband, Paul Bernardo, or whether she herself orchestrated, and enjoyed, much of the action.

Sociologists and criminologists are divided on the question of whether these crimes, and other high-profile violent crimes committed by women, are anomalies, or whether they signal a growing trend of women translating the greater equality they've achieved in the workplace and in the home to similar equality behind the knife and gun.

In fact, there is some evidence that young women *are* becoming more violent, and that women increasingly take the lead, rather than merely a secondary role, in violent crime. Though in recent years there have been declines in the rate of violent crimes, it is still higher than it was a decade ago. According to the Canadian Centre for Justice

sex in the snow

Statistics, the number of females charged with violent crimes under the Young Offenders' Act increased by over 500 per cent in the space of a decade. The rate of violent crime among adult women increased 130 per cent in the same period. The rates have also increased among young and adult men, but the proportional increases have not been as large: 325 per cent and 96 per cent, respectively. The pattern of greater increases in criminal activity among younger females than among older women was also reflected in the 1993 finding that adult women were charged with 11 per cent of the violent crimes committed by adults, but that young women were charged with 24 per cent of the violent crimes committed by youths.

Of course, drawing sweeping conclusions from crime statistics can be a rather slippery business. In regard to youth-crime statistics, for example, one has to be aware that some of the apparent increase in youth crime can be attributed to zero-tolerance policies (which result in youths being formally charged for misdemeanours that, in the past, might have been dealt with outside the court system). In addition, men continue to eclipse women in the commission of violent crimes by a long shot. There are a number of criminologists who believe that there is relatively little difference between the actual number and nature of crimes committed by today's youth and those committed in the past. In their view, the "increases" are more the result of changes in reporting procedures and policy decisions taken than any real change in the relative incidence rates in our society.

Besides violence, another area in which there are gender gaps between men and women in every age group is in perceptions of the social safety net, and the question of individual versus community responsibility for the care of those in need. Men are considerably more likely than women to believe in the survival of the fittest.

The decline of guilt and fear among young women is also reflected in the attitudes of young gays and lesbians who, unlike older homosexuals, tend to feel less guilty or anxious about their sexual preferences. As a result, they feel freer — and, in fact, *are* freer than in the past — to be open about their sexual orientation. (Nonetheless, even though homosexuality is no longer "the love that dares not speak its name," no one could realistically suggest that it does not take courage for a young man or woman to "come out of the closet.")

The decline of fear and guilt is not limited to the formerly disenfranchised. It is also apparent among some straight white men, with the emergence of so-called "angry white guys." In many ways, these men represent a backlash against society's overall tendency toward anti-authoritarianism. In their view — a view they no longer feel guilty about expressing — many straight white men charge governments and institutions with "caving in" to "special interest groups," at the expense of their rights and privileges. It's a view of the world based on the premise that there is a finite amount of "pie" to go around, and giving one person a larger "slice" means that someone else has to give up a bit of his share.

sex in the snow

Among the twelve tribes of Canadians, this viewpoint is most reflected in that of the Disengaged Darwinists. Members of this group score very low on trends related to egalitarianism, personal autonomy and multiculturalism. Their rejection of institutional authority is not a rejection of the idea of authority, but rather a rejection of what they see as "mosaic madness," of a watered-down "politically correct" heterarchy, and affirmative action and special programs for a never-ending list of minorities, all in the context of a government that continues to consume their tax dollars while delivering less and less of the social and economic security provided in the past. The fact that Caribana and the Gay Pride parade have replaced the Royal Agricultural Winter Fair and the Orange Parade as the biggest tourist draws to formerly white-bread Toronto is vexing in the extreme for Disengaged Darwinists, and their ideological forebears the Rational and Extroverted Traditionalists. The men in these segments are particularly aggrieved; imagine their intense ambivalence when Donovan Bailey won Olympic gold for Canada in the 100-metre dash.

Men, in addition to being more deferential to institutional authority, differ from women in their attitudes toward work. Women are more inclined than men to think that gaining personal satisfaction from one's job is as important as the pay cheque at the end of the month. For a number of reasons, men are considerably more oriented toward the bottom line. Traditionally, they've been better paid, and therefore get more satisfaction from the sheer heft of their pay cheques. They're also more accustomed to thinking of themselves as the main breadwinners in their families (still mostly, but not always, the reality).

In the 1950s and 1960s, the chances that a woman worked were inversely related to her husband's income, that is, the greater the husband's income, the less likely a wife would choose to work. Mothers of small children who did work risked the wrath of public opinion, and discrimination in the workplace and in post-secondary institutions that provided the necessary credentials for a professional career.

In those days, women worked because they had to work, often in low-paying female ghettos as secretaries, nurses or schoolteachers. Feminism opened up opportunities for women in more highly valued professions, and the result has been that the largest rise in working wives over the last twenty-five years has been in the upper end of the income scale, among women who live in families who do not necessarily "need" the income. Their motivation is as much personal fulfilment and meaningful employment (outside the home) as financial compensation. As in so many areas, a simplistic economic model of human behaviour misses the mark; values must be added to the calculus of motivation.

Beginning in the recent recession, we witnessed a rapid decline in the importance that Canadians — both men and women — attach to finding personal fulfilment through work. Strictly financial considerations became imperative. However, I predict that the quest for personally meaningful employment will regain importance, as Canadians become more inured to living with uncertainty, and less willing to defer emotional and spiritual gratification, even if it means some financial sacrifice.

Men and women also differ from each other on attitudes toward personal finances, and in the importance of aesthetics and ethics in the marketplace. Women are more likely than men to say that aesthetic criteria have a significant influence on their purchase decisions. Women are also more likely to say they would pay more for products that protect the environment, and that they would boycott companies that abuse human rights, are cruel to animals or destroy the environment. True to their traditional role as nurturers, women tend to express greater sympathy than men, not only for their immediate acquaintances, but for people in general and even for other life forms and the natural environment.

Our research finds that another cliché about men and women, namely, that men take a more rational, inner-directed approach to life and women a more emotional, outer-directed approach is largely true. Women continue to be more concerned than men with appearances, both their own and that of their surroundings. But, once again, it is not true to the extent that people believe. In terms of social values, far more significant than gender differences are generational differences: older Canadians, especially

Rational Traditionalists, attach significantly more importance to reason and logic, and less to intensity of emotions, than do the youth tribes. Among the youth — male
and female, gay and straight — intensity and passion are
where it's at.

Men are more likely than women to feel in control of their own
lives, and they also attach more importance to being
in control. They feel less rushed — in part because they
still assume fewer domestic responsibilities. They also
express slightly less concern than do women over their
future finances.

Both men and women attach great importance to fidelity
between partners and to the family in general, although
these sentiments are somewhat stronger among women.
In this area, however, generational differences are far more
significant than the relatively small differences between the
sexes. Younger Canadians, both male and female, are
much more liberal than their elders, and more sexually
freewheeling.

Women are more likely than men to embrace a broader
concept of family, one that includes common-law and
same-sex relationships. In every age group except the
oldest, women tend to be more accepting than men of
these non-traditional forms of family, though, once again,
generational and tribal differences are pronounced. For
example, three-quarters of Extroverted Traditionalists
oppose same-sex couples being accorded the same

rights as married couples; two-thirds of New Aquarians support the idea.

Whether it is a question of different cultures or different sexual orientations, women, especially young women, are considerably more at ease than are men with people who are different from themselves. For example, they are more likely than men to embrace the ideal of multiculturalism, and to view Canada as a mosaic rather than a melting pot. At a more intimate level, they exhibit greater flexibility in their own personality, including their gender identity: it is easier for a woman than it is for a man to admit to some-times feeling more "masculine" and, at other times, more "feminine." Women also feel it is important to be able to openly express their emotions to those with whom they are close, something that men in every age group are less like-ly to acknowledge. Young men, although among the most active and intense of Canadians, tend to be at a loss for words when it comes to their emotions.

On the other hand, men are more at ease with new experi-ences — as long as these don't involve an empathetic understanding or sympathizing with others. They are more likely than women to feel they're adaptable and comfortable with complexity; they are more confident of their ability to respond to changing circumstances. Nonetheless, differ-ences in adaptability among the twelve values tribes are far more pronounced than those between the sexes. For example, most Extroverted Traditionalists, whether male or female, say they hate new, unforeseen situations, but most

New Aquarians, male or female, say they welcome such challenges.

Men are significantly more likely than women to be techno-enthusiasts. As a general rule, the youth tribes are the first, and older Canadians the last, to adopt new technologies. However, our research suggests that the largest gender gap in enthusiasm for technology is among Canadians in their twenties and thirties, with the men being much more enthusiastic about technology than the women.

Perhaps this reflects the fact that computer software has been written largely by men, and that the gap between young men and women is parallel to that between English speakers and non-English speakers: so far, much software is just not available in their "language." There is some scientific evidence that the central processing units or "wetware" (brains) of men and women are wired slightly differently, and we have yet to invent (or at least widely disseminate) "female" software. The availability of French-language computer software is finally resulting in increasing rates of participation in the new media among francophones.

Men are much less attached than women to religion, or even to spirituality or rituals. In every age category, women are more religious than men. However, the greatest differences are found among older Canadians; increasingly, younger Canadians, both men and women, have simply abandoned organized religion. Interestingly, despite this apparent hard-headedness on the part of men, they are slightly more inclined than women to express interest in mysterious occult forces such as astrology or tarot cards, and to believe that some phenomena may simply defy scientific explanation. Younger men, in particular, are fascinated by the unknown, and young gay men are even more likely to harbour such a fascination. The New Aquarians, the tribe that includes the highest proportion of gays and lesbians, is also the most interested in non-traditional spirituality, such as neo-paganism or New Age ideas.

Our research suggests that, although there is some truth in the idea of a young gay male cult of the body, such a cult is as prevalent among young lesbians as among gay men. The notorious American cultural theorist Camille Paglia, a self-described "penis-loving lesbian," has suggested that gay culture is a noble culture of beauty and body worship, while lesbian culture is ugly and barren, devoid of beauty. So, are lesbians finally buying into the "beauty myth"? How, some will ask, can popular wisdom be so far off the mark? It appears that a number of small, questionable assumptions have contributed to a misperception.

Part of it, I think, can be attributed to the public's wilful or unconscious refusal to recognize that lesbians are in their midst. Particularly in the case of beautiful women, this resistance is fierce. When people see a beautiful woman, the tendency is to assume she is straight. And if a beautiful woman is seen touching, or even kissing, another woman, there is still a widespread assumption that she is

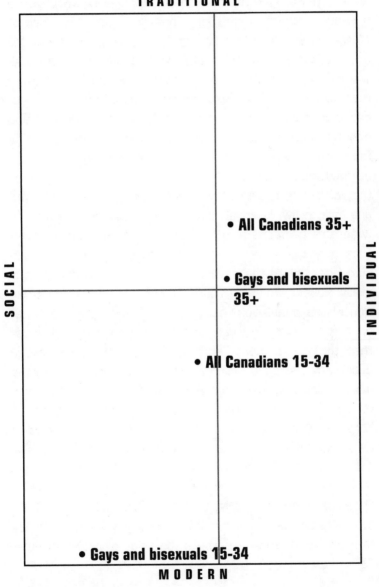

TRADITIONAL

SOCIAL

INDIVIDUAL

• All Canadians 35+

• Gays and bisexuals 35+

• All Canadians 15-34

• Gays and bisexuals 15-34

MODERN

Environics

straight. This perception is so firmly entrenched in popular consciousness, that many men will gladly watch porn movies or flip through magazines such as *Penthouse* or *Hustler* in which women are shown making love with each other, and they will still overwhelmingly assume that these women are straight. On the other hand, a man who so much as puts gel in his hair, sports an earring or two, or has dinner with another man is often suspected of being gay (though these assumptions are less frequent in Canada's largest cities). So, there may be a larger than acknowledged number of "lipstick lesbians" who, because they do not fit the traditional stereotype of the "ugly dyke," are able to live relatively openly and display their affection, with the general population nonetheless oblivious. Strangely, the public seems unable to see an attractive lesbian right before their eyes, yet ready to see a gay man in every closet. For the record, it appears that the proportion of the population that is gay is more than the 1 per cent figure favoured by conservatives, but considerably less than the 10 per cent estimate favoured by gay activists. Even with bisexuals included, the proportion is well under 10 per cent; we estimate about 5. Still enough, however, to achieve greater attendance at the Gay Pride parade in Toronto than in any other city in North America, including San Francisco — almost three-quarters of a million in 1996.

Older gays and bisexuals, who often felt guilty about their sexuality or fearful of coming out, largely adopted values that are very similar to others their age who are straight.

But today, four in ten Canadians are in favour of gay couples being treated the same as married couples, with the
progressive youth tribes being particularly supportive. This
greater acceptance by society has resulted in greater self-
acceptance by gays and bisexuals. Overall, young
Canadians are located in the lower left "experience-seeking
new communities" quadrant of the 3SC map. Young gays
and bisexuals are on the leading edge of this trend, cutting-
edge modern (or even post-modern): if they are not
already, they soon will be having sex in the snow.

8

CANADIANS AND AMERICANS: THE GARDEN AND THE JUNGLE

"If some countries have too much history, Canada has too much geography."

—William Lyon Mackenzie King

As countless commentators — most prominently the eminent sociologist Seymour Martin Lipset — have pointed out, historically, Canadians have been much more deferential to institutional authority than was the case among Americans. However, in the space of a single generation, Canadians have, for better or worse, by necessity and by choice, become much less deferential. On many registers we are now even more critical of institutional authority and of our élites than Americans are of theirs. Canadians can be likened to children on the last day of school, running and squealing in the schoolyard, free at last from the rules and discipline imposed by tradition. A nation of "repressed hedonists" — an apt description of our longest serving prime minister, quoted above — has decided that "peace, order and good government" is not enough, and, like citizens around the world, we want some of the "life, liberty and happiness" promised in America's founding declaration. For a very long time, Canadians lived under the not-always-benign rule of the church, the state and the large institutions of the industrial era — corporations, state monopolies and labour unions. Now we are freer to call the shots.

Since the 1960s, the widespread questioning of authority has become a fact of civic life in much of the Western world. However, Canada's evolution in this respect has been particularly rapid, to the point of being characterized as a "revolution" by Canada's pre-eminent journalist Peter C. Newman in his book *The Canadian Revolution: From Deference to Defiance*. Perhaps one reason for this is the Canadian surfeit of geography and dearth of history, as Mackenzie King observed half a century ago. As a result, no historical ideology has the sort of grip on our souls that the myth of the American Dream has south of the border. Even the Conquest (of Quebec by General Wolfe in 1759) has lost much of its resonance for Quebec francophones, thirty-five years after the Quiet Revolution. Instead, Canadians have a sort of flexible "geophilosophy," more pragmatic and rooted less in history and more in the multicultural, multimedia reality of their everyday existence. In today's wired world, both history and geography have lost most of their relevance for Canadians, in spite of the valiant efforts of the Charles R. Bronfman Foundation's Heritage Moments series of mini-docudramas. Today we have too much of neither, but perhaps instead have too little imagination to see ourselves as the world does — as the best place on earth.

Arguably, the relative lack of historical and ideological baggage has allowed Canadians to adapt rapidly to changing conditions both within our borders and around the world. It has also resulted in pronounced socio-cultural differences between Canadians and Americans in the roles they ascribe to the fundamental institutions of religion, state, family and the marketplace.

Despite their mythological adherence to the ideal of personal freedom, Americans, in fact, harbour a far greater confidence in many institutions than do Canadians. In general, Americans have a greater faith in the family, the state (that is, "America"), religion and the market.

For example, Americans express far greater confidence in big business. Part of this difference can be attributed to the fact that "big business" in the United States usually means *American* big business. In Canada, "big business" is often a foreign-owned corporation, typically an American branch plant. In America, anti-trust laws force fierce competition. In Canada, public-sector monopolies and private-sector oligopolies have dominated many markets; the result was a culture of *ressentiment* — resentful dependence — which began to unravel in the late 1980s.

But now, Canadians have become "masters of suspicion," with both the positive and negative aspects that come with such a posture. In spite of our historical reputation for deference to élites, Canadians, who were once more religious than Americans, are now less so. Although mere church attendance figures fail to do justice to the phenomenally greater religiosity in the United States, they do illustrate important differences between the two countries. As I noted at the outset of this book, in the 1950s, 60 per cent of Canadians attended church every Sunday; today, that number is 30 per cent. In the United States, attendance continues to hover around 40 per cent, little changed from the level found in the 1930s and '40s.

Even Quebecers, whose motto is *Je me souviens* (or "I remember"), have come to forget or reject a great deal of their socio-cultural inheritance. With the exception, of course, of the French language itself, almost every other institution in that centuries-old society has been turned upside down. In the space of a single generation, people who came from families of ten children are today having only one child, or sometimes none. The decline in weekly church attendance among Quebec Catholics has been even more precipitous than in the rest of the country.

One factor that initially contributed to greater *Canadian* religiosity and deference to authority was the historical role played by the major Christian denominations. Historically, in Canada, the Catholic and Anglican churches, both very hierarchical organizations, played a dominant role. And they did so with explicit or tacit government sanction, in part through the constitutional provisions which protected Catholic and Protestant denominational schools. In contrast, the American constitution separated church and state. Evangelical or populist sects had to compete for the attention and adherence of their American flocks, thereby giving religion a less institutional focus.

Historically, this difference favoured greater religiosity in Canada. However, with faith in institutions declining in both countries, the more heterarchical orientation of religion in the United States has proven the more resilient and "market sensitive." In Canada, most mainstream Judeo-Christian denominations are losing their grip on the population. Moreover, many of the values traditionally associated with them have come under critical scrutiny, if they have not been largely discarded. These include deference to state authorities ("render unto Caesar"), patriarchal definitions of family, guilt, duty, and fear of divine retribution.

Not only does our research show that Canadians are far weaker than Americans on the dimension of religiosity, but that the secularization of our country shows no signs of abating. If anything, this trend is accelerating. Despite a nominal separation of church and state in the United States, religion continues to play a major role in American politics, but virtually no role here. In this respect, the 49th parallel is a veritable "de-mystification zone." American politicians wear their religion on their sleeves; here, even the most devout politicians, including Reform Party leader

Preston Manning, seldom mention their religious affiliation and Christian values.

Even Canadians who say they believe in God — still a majority — tend not to let this belief influence their lifestyle on a day-to-day basis. When it comes to their religious practices, they are more likely to apologize than proselytize. Reginald Bibby, the foremost sociologist of religion in this country, comments that "The vast majority of Canadians still call themselves Christian, but they're grasping bits and pieces of the traditional creed — 'the fragmented god.' We now see a high level of belief in almost anything imaginable, but there's no rhyme or reason to it. And when we try to measure the sort of guidance these private beliefs play in people's lives, there's really nothing there. There's no ultimate moral authority. So it really doesn't add up to anything."[14]

On the other hand, four out of five Americans believe in life after death, a virgin birth and miracles. Almost all Americans (95%) believe in God, and a World Values survey conducted in 1990–93 found that more than four in five Americans consider themselves to be "a religious person."

In the United States, social or values issues can still play an important role in elections, inspiring US author Ben Wattenberg to recently write the influential *Values Matter Most*.[15] In Canada, it is unemployment and the deficit that are top public priorities in the late 1990s — both pragmatic economic issues. With tongue planted firmly in cheek, some Canadians have said the ultimate Canadian destiny is to redeem America. If this were ever to happen, it would be a secular redemption, a redemption from Redemption.

Just as Canadian religious institutions have suffered a greater decline in public confidence than have their American counterparts, so, too, has there been a greater decline in confidence in government here. Traditionally, Canadians had far greater faith in the state than did their American cousins. Much of this phenomenon can be traced to the very different origins of the two countries. In several books, most recently *American Exceptionalism*, Lipset examines the historical and cultural differences between Canada and the United States in the founding myths of each country: the revolutionary and individualistic tradition of the United States, contrasted with the counter-revolutionary and communal tradition of Canada; the American rags-to-riches myth of Horatio Alger versus the Canadian theme of surviving adversity; the American promise of life, liberty and the pursuit of happiness in contrast to the Canadian bargain of peace, order and good government. In terms of political ideology, Canada inherited strong strains of Toryism, liberalism and socialism. The United States has only known various strains of liberalism qualified by religious moralism.

Traditionally, Canada was very much a communitarian, or group-oriented society. According to Lipset, Canada's "organizing principle," our decision not to join the American Revolution in 1776 and break with England, left us with the values and priorities of the Old World, and an essentially Tory and conservative world-view. To restate the old joke: America was founded on the principle of the people against the government; Canada, on the other hand, was founded on the principle of the government against the people.

Old World Tory conservatism, which takes an organic, "Hegelian" view of society, sees the whole as greater than the sum of its parts and, as such, values group rights over individual rights. This particular world-view, along with the nation's climate, geography and smaller population, has made Canadians generally accepting of state intervention in many aspects of their daily lives. Many observers have remarked that Canada was traditionally a very "Hegelian" society, a label that applies to the country's pre-eminent political philosopher, Charles Taylor.

This organic view was reflected in Canadians' constantly trying to accommodate competing interests within the framework of existing social institutions, a profoundly reformist (rather than revolutionary) ambition. However, it has now become apparent to Canadians that traditional institutions can no longer deliver the goods: the church can no longer deliver ever-lasting life, the state can no longer provide security from the cradle to the grave, and employers can no longer guarantee life-long employment.

As these formerly unassailable institutions crumble, Canadians are forced to forge new links and networks with communities of choice and of mutual interest, rather than looking to government or other élites to lead them through life. With the growth of social-values tribalism and the underground economy, Canadians have moved from an organic model of society to a rhizomatic one, where personal networking replaces a reliance on representatives, institutions or an idealized notion of the country.

Our research shows that Americans, in addition to a greater religiosity, are characterized by a strong belief in the importance of national superiority, a romantic need to demonstrate to the world the exceptionalism of their country and culture. American Republicans have distilled these values into their purified essence.

The summer blockbuster of 1996, *Independence Day*, starts out as just such a paean to American exceptionalism. However, by the end of the film it has become an exhortation to global unity in a common cause, with everyone included, from the First Lady to a stripper with a heart of gold, from a black soldier to a Jewish intellectual, with a sympathetic portrayal of a gay character tossed in for good measure. In the end, the entire world unites, under American leadership, to defeat the aliens from outer space. It's appealing, because this sort of ecumenism is so obviously absent from the US body politic these days.

Unfortunately, the tendency of Americans to identify themselves as simply "Americans" rather than "hyphenated" Americans appears to have done little to strengthen the social fabric in the United States. Indeed, as we can see from our synthesis map of values, the attitudinal differences between Canada's "distinct society" Quebec and the rest of the country pale in comparison to those that exist among the major regions of the United States. It may be argued that Canadians' institutional recognition of social pluralism, including state-sponsored bilingualism and multiculturalism, has provided a vehicle for the expression of *some* aspirations of ethnic communities. This has not made them any less Canadian: in fact, it has helped to make them *quintessentially* Canadian. It is not an exclusive disjunction, in which one is *either* ethnic or Canadian: one can comfortably be both, and the very Canadian trend toward more flexible personalities and a diffused sense of identity suggests that the recognition of a multicultural, fluid and flexible reality need not encourage an ossified ethnic tribalism. Twenty-five years of public-opinion polling in Canada has taught me a seemingly paradoxical truth: Canadians feel *strongly* about their *weak* attachments to Canada, its political institutions and their fellow citizens. In other words, they feel strongly about the right to live in a society that allows its citizens to be detached from ideology and critical of organizations, and not to feel obliged to be jingoistic or sentimentally patriotic. Canadians' *lack* of nationalism is, in many ways, a distinguishing feature of the country. In the 1950s we said, "better dead than red." If you believe in an afterlife, maybe it's better to be dead, but Canadians are now too pragmatic to jeopardize their lives for any ideology.

Until recently more deferential to politicians, Canadians

have been rejecting the authority of political office in much more dramatic ways than have Americans. Witness the near annihilation of the federal Conservatives in the 1993 election, and the introduction of the parvenu Bloc Québécois and the Reform Party as the second and third parties in the House of Commons. Canada has maintained a turnout rate of around 75 per cent in elections. The United States, on the other hand, is becoming increasingly plutocratic, with the rich and vested interests presiding over a nation where fewer than half the citizens exercise their franchise in presidential elections. In the Congressional elections of 1994, fewer than one in five Americans actually voted for the Republicans, who never-theless took this "victory" as a mandate for sweeping change.

Despite their sometimes brutal individualism, Americans revere institutions as anchors for their values; Canadians are coming to see many of their institutions as ineffective or irrelevant. For example, Americans revere the office of President and consider it a "crisis of confidence" when the incumbent's approval rating falls below 40 per cent. For an extended period of time, former prime minister Brian Mulroney had an approval rating hovering around 10 per cent, a situation unheard of in the United States.

As I mentioned earlier, a frequently cited characteristic dis-tinguishing Canada from other countries is our institutional-ized tolerance of diversity. However, this policy, along with other sacred cows of government, has come under

increasing scrutiny. In an attack on Canada's policy of multiculturalism, Neil Bissoondath writes, "It may be that one
of the unstated desires behind the institution of multiculturalism was a wish to mark ourselves as different from the
United States: if they have a melting pot, then we'll have a
mosaic. If they ask immigrants to shrug off their past and
assume a new identity, we'll ask immigrants to conserve
their past and make it their only identity."[16] Mr.
Bissoondath goes on to charge that a failure to accept
each other "as simply Canadian" weakens the social fabric.

However, I believe that Canada's more receptive attitude to
ethnic diversity is *not* a case of an individual pretending to
be what he/she was in the past, but rather, the simple
recognition of differences that exist in the present. This
hypothesis is supported by the fact that, in Canada, there
is a correlation between support for multiculturalism and
modern trends (such as equality of the sexes) rather than
traditional trends (such as religiosity). Multiculturalism is a
"modern" trend, located in the lower half of the map, rather
than a "traditional" one that would be found near the top of
the map. And perhaps the most modern of Canadians, the
New Aquarians, are also the most supportive of ethnic
diversity.

As in so many other areas, multiculturalism in Canada will
likely evolve from a government program to some sort of
"market multiculturalism" that's more voluntaristic and
pragmatic than the current approach. For example, schools
might emphasize their racial and ethnic diversity to attract

students. Companies might promote multiculturalism in order to retain and attract both employees and customers. The average Canadian can savour the gastronomic and cultural diversity of Canada's global village.

Clearly, when compared to our hot-blooded cousins to the south, we conform to the shy and deferential stereotype: except when playing hockey, we are non-violent and courteous. We raise the tone at the end of sentences, transforming assertions into hypotheses so as not to give offence, often adding "eh" to emphasize our politeness. We will stop at Stop signs, even if no cars are in sight, and even if the sign says *Arrêt*.

Given these differences, is it any surprise that an international survey by a major condom manufacturer found that Americans have sex more often than any other people in the world, but that Canadians were the most likely to say that the pleasure of their partner was very important? If Americans are hot Dionysians having sex in the sun, Canadians are cool Apollonians having sex in the snow, with the need for pragmatism that entails: blankets, mukluks and a realization that we are in this together.

Many Canadians believe that the 1990s have witnessed a steadily increasing income gap between the "haves" and the "have-nots"; in fact, this is only true for *earned* income. When transfers to lower-income individuals in the form of unemployment insurance, welfare and old-age security are factored in, the overall income gap has remained fairly constant, but at a growing and unsustainable cost to government and the taxpayer. Therefore, as the *Globe and Mail*'s Bruce Little observes, even though the market will probably continue to produce an inequitable distribution of earned income, governments will be increasingly unwilling and unable to offset this chilling trend.[17] However, in spite of the general retreat of governments, most Canadians continue to cling, however tenuously, to the principle of a kinder, gentler society. This stands in stark contrast to the social Darwinistic ideology that is dominant in the United States. Theirs is a world in which the fittest flourish while others languish. It is government by *triage*, in which resources are allocated to those deemed most worthy of being saved, or, more likely, those who have enough political clout to make their voices heard — older, well-off Americans being at the top of the list.

Despite these fundamental differences, there are indications that Canadian politics are replicating some American — or rather, some international — trends. The Ontario election of 1995, which saw a massive legislative majority accorded Mike Harris's Conservatives, witnessed a revolt by largely white, middle-class voters — many were the Disengaged Darwinists in our analysis — against an NDP government that they saw as "squandering" their tax dollars on policies of "overly generous" state welfare and employment equity (affirmative action). They voted in favour of a tax cut for the wealthy and middle class, with little concern for the plight of the poor. As columnist Allan Fotheringham put it, "Score one for the angry white guys." Canadians may still believe that the quality of our social programs distinguishes us from the United States, but a significant proportion of the population has come to question the price we pay for this benefit.

There are heated debates as to whether the cuts currently under way across the country are the solution to our economic problems, or an ideological reaction to market pressures. James Laxer, a political science professor at York University, argues that while the Harris government is *for the rich*, it is not a government *of the rich* and was not elected by the rich.[18] While those in the highest income-tax brackets will benefit most from tax cuts, middle-class conservative supporters will benefit from "cultural benefits," i.e., hot button issues such as a hard line on punishing young offenders, and the scrapping of photo radar (the latter which may have inspired David Cronenberg's latest film *Crash*).

Part of the cultural benefits accruing to Disengaged Darwinists — opposed to multiculturalism and alternative family structures — is a feeling of ethnic and moral superiority. As *The Globe and Mail* put it in an article about the United States, but which could be equally applied to sentiments now evident in neo-conservative Ontario, "the big dogs are suddenly fed up with blacks, gays, immigrants and everyone else that isn't them. Throughout the land can be heard the creaking sound of drawbridge politics, as the no-longer-silent majority try to isolate themselves in the duchies of suburbia."[19] For his part, Laxer suggests that the Harris agenda reflects the theory wittily and ironically summed up by John Kenneth Galbraith that, "the problem with our society is that the poor have too much money, and the rich don't have enough."

In my opinion, analyzing the election of the Ontario Conservatives in terms of the Americanization of Canadian politics is only telling part of the story. I interpret this vote as an effort by Ontarians to reverse some of the excesses — however well-intended — of state intervention, and to restore fiscal responsibility to the public sector. The mid-1990s have seen governments of all political stripes — Liberal in Ottawa, New Democratic in Saskatchewan, Conservative in Alberta and the PQ in Quebec — adopt many of the same fiscal and social policies. In 1996, in British Columbia, a slightly more interventionist New Democratic government was re-elected. Sure, there is some evidence of the Americanization of Canadian politics — after all, the plurality did vote in favour of free trade in 1988 — but there is just as much evidence that all Canadian governments are reducing services *reluctantly* and with little of the ideological fervour of the American right.

Canadians, I am convinced, are pragmatic, not ideological, people. They want a sustainable social-welfare state, perhaps not the social-democratic paradise envisioned by the Canadian left, but one which will still leave Canada a more egalitarian place than the republic to the south. It is no accident that other social-welfare states reacted to globalization in much the same manner as Canada: look at

Germany or New Zealand or what was once socialist heaven on earth — Sweden. They all bit the fiscal bullet.

The socio-cultural differences between Canada and the United States, like the differences between Quebec and the rest of Canada, or even between men and women, may be diminishing over time, but the differences that remain will, in my view, be significant and meaningful for many generations to come.

In order to better understand those differences, let us now turn to the 3SC analysis of *American* social values. In this case, the socio-cultural analysis is plotted on a North American "map of values." The North American map has different axes, because the trends appear in different locations on the US map, that is, the correlations among the trends are different: thus we have individuality versus conformity, and hedonism versus moralism. The map is divided into quadrants, allowing for comparisons to be made between Canada and the United States in terms of both general orientation and specific trends.

In the upper-left quadrant, *Ideals and Individualism*, are persons, groups and markets that have attained the classic, mostly material, version of the American Dream and have then integrated this affluence with liberal, personalized values.

In the upper-right quadrant, *Faith and Frustration*, are those whose outlook can be characterized as one part faith in a

The American Socio-Cultural Map

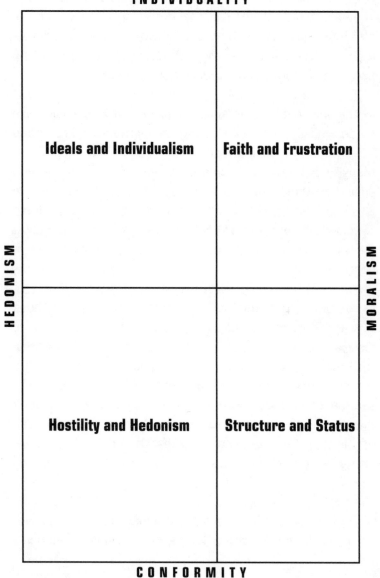

INDIVIDUALITY

Ideals and Individualism

Faith and Frustration

HEDONISM

MORALISM

Hostility and Hedonism

Structure and Status

CONFORMITY

Environics

higher order and institutions, and one part frustration at what they see as the erosion of the ideals they hold dear. They are true believers in the American Dream, but the strain of living with a shaky economy and uncertain employment has led them to worry that the Dream is slipping away, if not from them, at least from their children.

In the lower-left quadrant, *Hostility and Hedonism*, are those whose values can be characterized as "hard-edged hedonism" and a kind of conformist ethnic tribalism. Many in this quadrant have lower levels of education and socio-economic status. For them, the American Dream is something to be resented rather than coveted. Short of resorting to crime or vaulting into professional sports, the Dream is completely inaccessible to them, and obviously so.

In the lower-right quadrant, *Structure and Status*, are those whose orientation to life is characterized by rigid moralism, discipline and doing what's expected. Like the denizens of the *Hostility and Hedonism* quadrant, people in the *Structure and Status* quadrant tend to be from the lower socio-economic echelons of society. However, although they are just as unlikely to see the American Dream realized in their lives — for many, it exists only on their television screens — they revere it all the same.

The US Census Bureau divides the continental US into nine regions. New England includes Maine, New Hampshire, Vermont, Massachusetts, Rhode Island and Connecticut.

The Mid-Atlantic region comprises New York, Pennsylvania and New Jersey. The South Atlantic consists of Delaware, Maryland, Virginia, West Virginia, North Carolina, South Carolina, Georgia and Florida.

The East North Central (Midwest) region includes Michigan, Indiana, Ohio, Illinois and Wisconsin. The East

North American Geographical Regions

South Central (Deep South) region comprises Kentucky, Tennessee, Alabama and Mississippi. The West North Central (Plains) consists of Minnesota, Iowa, Missouri, Kansas, Nebraska, South Dakota and North Dakota.

The West South Central (Texarcana) region includes Arkansas, Louisiana, Texas and Oklahoma. The Mountain region comprises Montana, Wyoming, Colorado, New Mexico, Nevada, Arizona, Utah and Idaho. The West (Pacific) consists of Washington, Oregon and California (as well as Alaska and Hawaii).

According to our 3SC socio-cultural analysis, the "average" Canadian (an abstraction) is located in the upper left-hand quadrant of the North American map of values, the quadrant defined by the mental posture characterized as *Ideals and Individualism*. The "average" American (another abstraction) is located in the lower right-hand quadrant, a quadrant defined by the mental posture characterized as *Structure and Status*. This means that the average Canadian is stronger than the average American on the values of individuality and refined (or idealistic) hedonism; the average American is stronger on values that are conformist and moralistic. Interestingly, the values of Canadians most closely approach those of coastal Americans; the North-east (Boston and New England) and the North-west (San Francisco, Seattle) and their hinterlands.

Though there are regional differences in both Canada and

the United States, both English Canada and Quebec find themselves in the *Ideals and Individualism* quadrant of the North American map, together with the Pacific, New England and Plains regions of the United States. The Mountain region of the US is located in the *Faith and Frustration* quadrant, while the Midwest, South Atlantic and Deep South are in the *Structure and Status* quadrant. In the *Hedonism and Hostility* quadrant are the Mid-Atlantic and Texarcana regions.

It is clear from the socio-cultural data that, in spite of the many obvious similarities between the two countries, there are a number of significant differences in the values that guide and give meaning to the lives of people in each society. The first is in the flexibility we allow ourselves in terms of self-identity.

We Canadians are not without national pride. However, we question the assumption that national identity is the defining characteristic of community. This has afforded us a greater acceptance of diversity in each other's sense of self, and in the attachments people have with various communities. Here you are allowed, not only to be a hyphenated Canadian, but to decide which side of the hyphen best describes and defines you from moment to moment. A sort of pragmatic tolerance is the rule, rather than a clearly defined identity dictated by tradition. America, on the other hand, has a firm tradition of rejecting, or ghettoizing, hyphenated identities, in favour of one strong national identity.

INDIVIDUALITY

★ Mountain

★ New England

★ Pacific

❧ English Canada

★ Plains

❧ Quebec

HEDONISM

MORALISM

★ Midwest

★ South Atlantic

★ Mid-Atlantic

★ Deep
South

★ Texarcana

CONFORMITY

Environics

Is this because America was conceived, torn asunder and then reunited within a crucible of violence? In Canada, we negotiated our independence from Mother England. After their conquest in 1759, the British accommodated the French, starting with the Quebec Act in 1774. Allowing Quebecers to keep their language and customs, rather than pursue the course of assimilation, set a precedent for the non-violent accommodation of successive waves of immigrants. More recently, and thanks partly to the Charter of Rights and Freedoms, this same inclusiveness has opened up new possibilities for women, gays and lesbians, the disabled and others wishing to "immigrate" into the mainstream of society.

Canadians' recent questioning and criticism of their institutions has also resulted in more flexible and open personal relationships than is the norm in the United States. In my opinion, our questioning of the family has not resulted in its devaluation, but rather in an assault on patriarchy, and a greater belief in the equality of women and young people. It has also resulted in a more flexible definition of family, including a greater acceptance of non-Scriptural relationships, such as sex outside of marriage, and gay and lesbian relationships. Now one-third of children in Canada are born to parents who are living together but not married, and less than half of Canadian families conform to the traditional model of married-parents-with-kids. Jean Dumas, an analyst at Statistics Canada remarked, "There is a real change, not only in the size of the family, but in the concept of the family. The flexibility with which the cell of society adapts to societal change is amazing. All the talk about the death of the family is nonsense."[20]

In America, common-law marriage and the birth of children out of wedlock is interpreted as a sign of moral decay and the disintegration of society. The religious and political right inveigh against such trends with routine moralizing. In Canada overall, the trend goes essentially unnoticed in politics and is as much a marketing challenge as a moral threat to mainstream churches. North of the border, unmarried couples are becoming the norm, with formerly Catholic Quebec in the vanguard. However, there is antagonism among some of Canada's older values tribes on these questions.

In the United States, gender is now a major factor in Americans' political ideology and party choice. Women tend to support "kinder and gentler" policies that preserve the social-welfare state, and have thus become the backbone of the Democratic party. Men opt for a more competitive free-market economic model and Darwinistic social policies and are making the Republicans into a stag party. In America, it seems, "Men are from Mars and Women are from Venus."

In Canada, the ideological and partisan gap is far less pronounced. Yes, we see the tendency of women to be more on "the left" and men on "the right" of the political spectrum, but only a tendency. Canada's governing party, the Liberals, are slightly more popular among women than among men, but only slightly. Both the "left-wing" NDP, and the "right-wing" Progressive Conservatives draw similar levels of support from men and women. The further right-of-centre Reform Party is disproportionately male, but in Canada, unlike the United States, this positioning has served to limit Reform's appeal among mainstream male voters.

Further evidence of the advanced evolution of Canadian social values in the area of institutionalized gender stereo-typing is the fate of the Miss Canada Beauty Pageant. Though nearly every US state, county and town continues the ritual display of nubile female pulchritude, culminating in the annual Miss America and the redundant Miss Universe contests, Canada's CTV television network can-celled the Miss Canada contest in 1992 due to lack of interest on the part of sponsors and the general public. Meanwhile, in Texas, a related parody of Americana was played out when the mother of a would-be cheerleader, Wanda Webb Holloway, was convicted of plotting the death of the mother of her daughter's rival.

In addition to allowing for common-law and same-sex rela-tionships, the Canadian redefinition of the family has result-ed in a greater respect for the opinions of young people. One of the differences that distinguishes Canadian values from American is Canadians' greater adherence to the idea of an equal relationship with youth. Canadians are more egalitarian than Americans and more inclined to believe that young people are capable of making their own deci-

sions, and should be accorded the same rights and responsibilities as any other member of society.

Americans, on the other hand, are more likely than
Canadians to believe that young people do not really know
what is in their best interest, and that they should let their
elders tell them what to do. It is significant that in Canada,
there is a positive correlation between rejection of authority and belief in an equal relationship with youth; in the
United States these trends are independent of each other.
Certainly it makes intuitive sense that a rejection of hierarchical relationships in general would include those based on
age. So, why has this not happened in the US? Our data
suggest that the answer may lie in the fact that in both
countries people fear that permissive attitudes toward
young people may facilitate criminal behaviour. The greater
fear of crime in the US is reflected in a much harsher,
more authoritarian attitude toward the young, one now
realized in public curfews for youth and/or other exclusion-
ary measures.

Another distinguishing characteristic of Canadians is our
tendency toward non-violence. Canadians value peace and
order and will likely continue to do so, even without a
Mountie standing over their shoulder. Americans value
freedom of the individual more than peace and order.

Despite public perceptions to the contrary, Canadian statistics show a decline in rates of violent crime that paral-
lels a decline found in the United States. Statistics Canada

reported that in 1995 the overall crime rate fell by 1 per
cent, a decline for the fourth year in a row. Violent crime
declined by 4.1 per cent in 1995, the largest drop since
the agency started gathering such statistics in 1962.[21] In
1995, the homicide rate also hit a twenty-six-year low.
(Despite this overall decline, Statistics Canada reported
that there was an increase in the number and proportion of
murders committed by youth.)

The decline in overall crime rates in Canada and the US are
due, at least partly, to the demographic reality of aging
populations. This same demographic factor also helps
explain why there is a higher level of hysteria over crime —
older people tend to have a much greater fear of violence
than do the young.

For their part, Americans express somewhat contradictory
views on the topic of violence. On the one hand, they are
more likely than Canadians to accept violence as normative,
and even exciting, and are reluctant to institute the most
modest of gun-control measures. At the same time, crime
has long been one of the main issues of concern to the
American public.

Violent-crime rates peaked in the United States in 1990,
with the arrival of crack cocaine. In more recent years,
there has been a decline in the rate of violent crime in
the US. This can be attributed to a number of factors,
including lower rates of crack use, the death or impris-
onment of many of the worst offenders, and, as I just

pointed out, an aging population. Nonetheless, the United States is far from being out of the woods, especially in view of recent social program cuts and an imminent "echo boom" of teenagers and young adults, the age groups most likely to commit crimes. In the United States (and, to a lesser extent, in Canada) it is expected that violent crime will increase in the years ahead, simply because of a significant rise in the fifteen-to-twenty-four-year-old population. Demography may not be destiny, but in this instance it is a wake-up call of sorts, especially in the United States.

In the United States, people who murder strangers have an 80 per cent chance of getting away with it. It is a small step from recognition of this to a cost/benefit analysis on the part of those who, economically and socially, have little to lose by taking a chance on a life of crime. This is particularly true of those Americans in the *Hostility and Hedonism* quadrant.

And despite recent declines, the violent-crime rate in the United States remains many times higher than in Canada. Tom Pollock, head of Universal Pictures, pointed to Canada as evidence that there is not a correlation between on-screen violence and real-life violence. "We have a perfect control group," he said. "It's called Canada. They get all our records, movies and TV, yet their rate of violent crime is one-tenth that of the US. Toronto is on the other side of the lake from Buffalo but a world apart. What Canada has that we don't is strict gun control ... as well as less racial polarization and multi-generational poverty. Those are the real causes of violence."[22]

Both American and Canadian value systems are being shaped by the globalization of technology, trade, travel, finance, communications and culture. Some people believe that these broad contextual trends are acting to homogenize our values and lifestyles, and it *is* true that Canadians consume massive amounts of American popular culture. But we are not alone in this: on the other side of the Atlantic, even the proud and ethnocentric French now watch more American movies than those made in their own country.

The similarities in the way we live are legion, from the food we eat to the cars we drive, and in our social-values research we see broad similarities in the evolution of our values from conformity to traditional codes (order, authority, Judeo-Christian morality and attendant guilt) to more personalized, experiential values, with no theological pretensions or claims to universal validity. This pattern is particularly pronounced among the youth tribes.

In each country, baby boomers were in the vanguard of the new values: the quest for personal autonomy and self-fulfilment, the values most associated with the "Me Generation." Feminism, which was part of this search for autonomy and self-fulfilment, continues to be a strong trend in both countries, despite a backlash by those seeking to turn back the clock. So, too, is the trend away from asceticism and deferred gratification to hedonism and immediate gratification. On both sides of the border, people want to join the party, and have as much fun as possible on the roller coaster of life. They are less willing to wait for their ultimate reward in the next life (though Americans, much more than Canadians, continue to find comfort in the prospect of a more exalted world beyond death's door).

Individualism has been a growing trend in both the United States and Canada since the 1950s. However, our data indicate an important difference between the American and Canadian orientations to individualism: the American orientation can be characterized as "rugged individual-ism" and the Canadian version is more "responsible" than rugged. Ame-rican individualism is more competitive. Our values research finds that Americans are much more likely than Canadians to embrace a sense of per-sonal and national vitality and the stimulation of personal challenge; they are also more likely to admit to feelings of stress in the pursuit of success.

North of the 49th parallel, we treasure equality; south of it, they treasure freedom. Lipset points out that, historically, the United States also laid claim to being the land of equality of opportunity, with Canada being the land of élite accom-modation of group interests. However, it appears to me that Canada is now more egalitarian than the United States, and that Americans continue to cling tenaciously to a myth of social mobility that, in reality, holds for only a small propor-tion of their population. For example, in Canada the richest 1 per cent of the population holds about 25 per cent of the nation's wealth; in the United States the richest 1 per cent holds over 40 per cent of the wealth.[23]

Despite many signs that the United States is fast becoming a hereditary oligarchy, the ideal of social mobility — the belief that through education and hard work, anyone can rise to the top — remains a key component of the American Dream. There is insufficient recognition that growing proportions of Americans are born, not only into poverty, but also into hopelessness. To borrow Lord Durham's description of Canada in 1840, the United States is once again becoming two nations "warring within the bosom of a single state," only this time it is the rich versus the poor, with levels of violence approaching that of America's Civil War in the 1860s.

Even among the disadvantaged echelons of society, the American orientation to life is more judgmental and moralistic than is the Canadian. The American moral code is more firmly rooted in Judeo-Christian doctrine, a Manichean world of good and evil, right and wrong, good guys and bad guys, Eve created out of man's rib, and Adam created in the image of God and given dominion over the natural world. Canadian morality transcends traditional religious definitions; it can be characterized as a secular, pluralistic and ecological morality, a greater responsibility for the other. The Canadian emphasis on egalitarian values goes beyond the equality of human beings — whatever their sex, age, race, ethnicity or sexual orientation — to the consideration of non-human species and the natural environment. I expect this principle will be codified in the preamble the next time we amend the Canadian constitution. Canada's global village is a global garden.

It is my opinion that, although economic integration continues apace, there has been much less socio-cultural assimilation of Canada by the United States than is often feared. In important ways, Canadians and Americans live different sorts of lives. Moreover, I predict such assimilation will not take place for many generations to come, if ever. Though our economic axis has become north-south, our cultural axis has become, like our population, cybernomadic. Whereas television was initially a force that helped create mass society and popular culture, the new technologies of VCRs, satellite TV and the Internet all contribute to a socio-cultural fragmentation of mass society in favour of personal choice and empowerment. Common ideals and even "common sense" are increasingly hard to maintain, and the American national motto — *"e pluribus unum"* — or *"out of many, one"* — has turned out to be a tragic joke. It is truly ironic that Canada, a country that historically accommodated and even celebrated differences, has actually ended up creating a culture where a broad range of values unites us, and differentiates us significantly from Americans. On the other hand, the United States, in its drive to create a melting pot that disparages cultural and linguistic diversity, has, in fact, developed into a country of mutually exclusive identities and many warring factions. They have become a nation of god-fearing Darwinists, we have become a collection of tolerant social democrats.

Many people see social fragmentation and tribalism on the rise around the world, and the United States reverting to the *ethnic* tribalism of the past. Others, like Francis Fukuyama and Gwynne Dyer see more sanguine, hopeful trends. If my reading of Canada is correct, this country may be the harbinger of a more utopian future, as we experience an evolution from traditional ethnic tribalism to a post-modern tribalism based on social values.

In fact, despite tribal differences, French and English Canadians have far more in common with each other in terms of values than either group has with the Americans (however offensive this observation might be to political ideologues of the "distinct society"). Notwithstanding the Quiet Revolution in Quebec and the Values Revolution in Canada as a whole, Canadians themselves are not revolutionaries: they are rebels and reformers. And in spite of our growing intimacy with American commerce and culture, Canada remains a distinct society on the northern half of the North American continent.

Even in the face of powerful international forces favouring integration, our roots, our history, our size, our degree of secularization, our institutions and yes, even our climate have created two very different socio-cultural environments on this continent. If we are the kinder, gentler society of level playing fields, then America is the land of shining cities, each surrounded by a walled moat outside of which roams a marauding and dangerous underclass. In their own minds, most Canadians have decided which model they prefer: an overwhelming majority say they would choose to remain in Canada even if they had equal opportunities in the United States.

Postface

UTOPIA OR DYSTOPIA?

"She was back in Skinner's room, reading *National Geographic* about how Canada split itself into five countries."
— William Gibson in *Virtual Light*

Will Canada split up? Is the country getting better or worse? Are we evolving into an idealistic utopia in which Canadians achieve a new sense of community, one less parochial than in the past, but which still unites us? Or are we descending into a jungle of social Darwinism and fragmentation?

These questions preoccupy Canadians, whether at the Saturday-evening dinner table or in the editorial pages of our newspapers. On the surface, much appears to be going wrong. Some Quebecers threaten to blow up the federation. The country is mired in debt. Our beloved social safety net has been strained, almost beyond capacity, where it is not already torn. Young people can't find jobs, and even those who are employed fear they will be the next victims of corporate or government downsizing.

Polls show Canadians to be in a constant state of anxiety,

as they rationalize their eroding living standards and adjust to declining expectations, only occasionally interrupted by moments of relief and relaxation.

But the deeper evolution of social values tells a different story. It tells us of a people who are assuming more personal control over their own lives and are no longer relying on others (their parents, their spouse, their boss, or the corporate, political and religious establishments) to take care of them and lead them into the future. Whether they sought it or simply were forced to accept the inevitable, Canadians are finding that they are largely on their own. Increasingly, their lives and opportunities are being shaped by their own attitudes and the voluntary associations, networks and projects they initiate themselves. They are on their own, but not alone. Some would say this is the liberal democratic ideal; not just for white men who own property, but for everyone. Everyone, that is, with an adaptable mental posture and a skill-set to navigate life's myriad challenges.

I have made the case that demography is not necessarily destiny. At the same time, there is no denying our mortality and the inevitable passage of some of our fellow Canadians each year into the next world. Not all, but most of these people will be older, and harbour the traditional values characteristic of their generation. In twenty-five years, the post-war baby boomers will comprise the bulk of Canada's senior citizens. The present-day Gen Xers will be middle-aged, and my kids, Marion and Willie, will be students in some sort of

virtual university, or engaged in a project on another continent or planet.

What kind of a country will we have, when the values of
today's youth are dominant? A world transformed by Gen
Xers and technology as dramatically as boomers and television have transformed ours. Remember, in Canada, this
will be a world of New Aquarians, Autonomous Post-
Materialists, Social Hedonists, Thrill-seeking Materialists
and Aimless Dependents. Though they may become more
traditional as they grow older, they will not return to the
traditionalism of their predecessors. The Cosmopolitan
Modernists have shown us that people do not inevitably
become conservative or reactionary in their old age. And
just as the Cosmopolitan Modernists are "smelling the
roses" in their old age, their Autonomous Rebel successors
can be expected to do the same. The opportunities for
experiential travel, learning and cultural exploration will be
boundless, as will new ways of defining life's meaning and
its rituals for a generation coming to terms with its mortality. I'm sorry, but *Death in the Snow* is the inevitable
sequel, folks.

The present era has been dominated by the defining segment of the baby boomers, the Autonomous Rebels, and
their predecessors, the Cosmopolitan Modernists. These
groups are now being challenged, and pessimists would say
have already been defeated, by the Disengaged Darwinists
and their older counterparts, the Rational Traditionalists.
Battles are being waged by these groups on the stage of

politics in each election or referendum, and within our institutions and corporate organizations on a daily basis.

Twenty years from now, the battles will be waged among
today's youth tribes. In some ways, the New Aquarians
and Autonomous Post-Materialists will follow in the foot-
steps of the Autonomous Rebels and Cosmopolitan
Modernists; in other ways, they will blaze new trails we can
only imagine. Will they be the wired post-nationalists
endeavouring to maintain peace, order and what's left of
government? Or will peace and order be displaced by chaos
and contingency, and government be as (ir)relevant as
mainstream religion is today?

In any case, the "progressive" tribes will face reactionary,
and sometimes dangerous opponents — many of whom will
be Aimless Dependents and Thrill-seeking Materialists —
still looking for a leader, an ideology and a god. The lives of
the more marginal members of these tribes will often be
nasty, brutish and shorter, because they will be the losers
in a world in which the safety net has many holes, if it
exists at all.

Few envisioned the impact of OPEC on the 1970s, of globalization on the 1980s, or the Internet on the 1990s. The
great futurist Herman Kahn foresaw the rise of Japan, but
did not foresee the limitations its culture would place on its
ability to adapt to the values of individual autonomy and
hedonism. So too may the pessimistic futurists be wrong
about Canada, its inevitable fragmentation and absorption

into the US. I personally envision another scenario, one of autonomy and interdependence, a pragmatic balance that is my reading of our historical evolution from day one.

What does the future hold for us? Will Canada successfully make the transition from the traditional institutions of the past (upper-left quadrant) to modern, less parochial communities (lower-left quadrant)? Or will it hurtle toward some sort of nihilistic social Darwinism (at the far right of the map), where, as philosopher Mark Kingwell observes, the rich are "*piñatas* in need of a clubbing"? Or, as in the minds of Canada's left, will the poor, thrown off social assistance, be forced to rent themselves out as *piñatas* at birthday parties for the children of the rich?

When answering this question of what the future holds, we should be clear as to what is at stake: the number two economy in the Organization of American States; the number two economy in the British Commonwealth; the number two economy in *la francophonie*; and what the UN calls the best quality of life in the world. Like Blanche Dubois, whom I quoted in the introduction, we Canadians have "riches of the spirit" we are only beginning to become aware of or admit to.

When I look at the evolution of Canadian social values, I see a future in which multiple personalities will be expressed within the same individual, allowing him or her to form new communities, corporate entities and networks, both present and virtual, with other Canadians, with others around the world, and with the natural environment. The evolution of social values in Canada is a winding journey from the death of God and traditional notions of family and community, to a highly individualistic population focused on personal control and autonomy, to a now embryonic but fast-growing sense of human interconnectedness with technology and nature. These developments, I believe, are natural extensions of our efforts to transcend the traditional demographic characteristics that defined and often limited the paths we followed in our lives. I believe we are at the dawn, not the end of civilization.

I envision a Canada in twenty years that is closer to the United States economically, and yet culturally distinct. I see a Quebec that is economically closer to the rest of Canada and to the United States, yet culturally distinct. To the cynic, the differences may seem trivial, but to the people living in these communities, these differences will be important elements of their flexible, fluid, ever-changing self-image.

In Canada, the élites and people who have a fetish for clean, neat and permanent solutions want a rational, and much more decentralized, division of powers than was envisioned by the Fathers of Confederation. However, there is little reason to believe Canadians would be any more satisfied with such a devolution of power than they are with the current arrangement. Perhaps workable in the distant past, the idea of bringing representative government "closer to the people" is destined to disappoint, because "the people" are already elsewhere, with attachments to a diversity of communities other than simply the locale in which they live. If demography is no longer destiny, then ultimately neither are history or geography.

Of course Quebec is distinct, but so too is Newfoundland or British Columbia. Even Ontarians are distinct. The point is ... we are all distinct, all 30 million of us, whatever our race, religion or region. And increasingly, that distinctiveness is our own creation, not the arbitrary category someone else invented, but our own blending of the inevitable and the possible.

In my view, efforts to chisel new political platitudes in marble are destined to fail in a world of endless editing on the personal computer, ever-evolving relationships and perpetual change. In such a context, "fixed" identities and "final" solutions are for madmen. Canada is about accommodating differences between ourselves and *within* ourselves: men and women, rich and poor, French and English, black and white, straight and gay. We either accommodate and become bigger, or segregate and become smaller, literally and emotionally.

If I had to guess, I would put my money on the New Aquarians and Autonomous Post-materialists as the defining tribes of their generation in twenty-first-century Canada. Already on the leading edge of modern values, they will be the multicultural crew on the bridge of our "Starship Enterprise."

Canada's Social Values Tribes

The Elders

COSMOPOLITAN
MODERNISTS
20%

RATIONAL
TRADITIONALISTS
54%

EXTROVERTED
TRADITIONALISTS
26%

RATIONAL TRADITIONALISTS

Key Demographics

POPULATION
- Proportion mf Canadian population: 15 per cent
- Proportion of Canadians 50 years of age or older: 54 per cent
- Total number in Canada: 3.5 million

OTHER DEMOGRAPHICS
- Higher than average proportion in communities of less than 5000 people

Fundamental Motivation

- Financial Independence, Stability and Security

Key Values
- Religiosity
- Primacy of Reason
- Respect for Historical Tradition
- Respect for Authority
- Duty
- Guilt
- Deferred Gratification

Words to Live By

- "Follow your head, not your heart"
- "Better safe than sorry"
- "A bird in the hand is worth two in the bush"
- "A woman's place is in the home"
- "Father knows best"
- "Beauty is only skin deep"

Icons

- Former British prime minister Winston Churchill
- Situation comedy character *Ward Cleaver*
- Former businessman and politician C.D. Howe
- Former American president Franklin D. Roosevelt

EXTROVERTED TRADITIONALISTS

Key Demographics

POPULATION
- Proportion of Canadian population: 7 per cent
- Proportion of Canadians 50 years of age or older: 26 per cent
- Total number in Canada: 1.7 million

OTHER DEMOGRAPHICS
- Higher than average proportion live in Quebec or the Maritimes
- Higher than average proportion are women

Fundamental Motivation

- Traditional Communities, Institutions and Social Status

Key Values
- Religiosity
- Family
- Respect for Historical Tradition
- Respect for Institutions
- Duty
- Fear
- Deferred Gratification

Words to Live By
- "Duty above all else"
- "A woman's work is never done"
- "Family comes first"
- "A penny saved is a penny earned"
- "Spare the rod and spoil the child"
- "Adam and Eve, not Adam and Steve"

Icons
- Prime Minister Jean Chrétien
- Former Quebec premier Maurice Duplessis
- Jesus Christ
- Actress Harriet Nelson from "Ozzie and Harriet"
- Activist for the poor Mother Teresa

COSMOPOLITAN MODERNISTS

Key Demographics

POPULATION
- Proportion of Canadian population: 6 per cent
- Proportion of Canadians 50 years of age or older: 20 per cent
- Total number in Canada: 1.4 million

OTHER DEMOGRAPHICS
- Higher than average proportion live in British Columbia
- Higher than average proportion are in their 50s
- Higher than average proportion have post-secondary education

Fundamental Motivation
- Traditional Institutions and Experience-seeking

Key Values
- Global World-view
- Respect for Education
- Desire for Innovation

Words to Live By
- "The world is my oyster"
- "Progress is our most important product"
- "Take time to smell the roses"
- "Think globally, act locally"

Icons
- Writer Pierre Berton
- Former govenor-general Jeanne Sauvé
- Business leader Maurice Strong
- Former prime minister Pierre Trudeau

The Boomers

**DISENGAGED
DARWINISTS
41%**

**AUTONOMOUS
REBELS
25%**

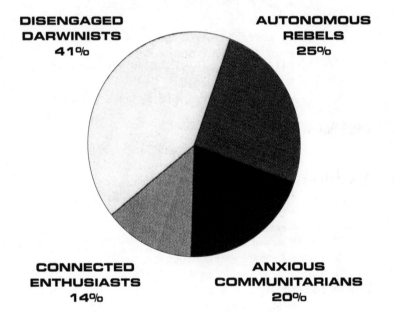

**CONNECTED
ENTHUSIASTS
14%**

**ANXIOUS
COMMUNITARIANS
20%**

AUTONOMOUS REBELS

Key Demographics

POPULATION
- Proportion of Canadian population: 10 per cent
- Proportion of Canadians 30 to 49 years of age: 25 per cent
- Total number in Canada: 2.4 million

OTHER DEMOGRAPHICS
- Higher than average proportion in Vancouver
- Higher than average incomes
- Higher than average proportion have post-secondary education
- Higher than average proportion are professionals

Fundamental Motivation
- Personal Autonomy and Self-Fulfilment

Key Values
- Strong Belief in Human Rights
- Scepticism toward Traditional Institutions
- Suspicion of Authority
- Freedom
- Individuality
- Respect for Education

Words to Live By
- "Knowledge is Power"
- "To each her own"
- "I did it my way"
- "The personal is political"

Icons
- American president Bill Clinton and his wife Hillary
- Singer John Lennon
- *Scully* and *Mulder* from "The X-Files"
- Writer and feminist leader Gloria Steinem

ANXIOUS COMMUNITARIANS

Key Demographics

POPULATION
- Proportion of Canadian population: 9 per cent
- Proportion of Canadians 30 to 49 years of age: 20 per cent
- Total number in Canada: 2.1 million

OTHER DEMOGRAPHICS
- Higher than average proportion in small or mid-sized communities
- Higher than average proportion in the Prairie provinces
- Higher than average proportion are women

Fundamental Motivation

- Traditional Communities, Institutions and Social Status

Key Values
- Family
- Community
- Fear
- Duty
- Need for Respect

Words to Live By
- "Our children are our future"
- "If everyone did their share it would be a better world"
- "We are our brother's keeper"
- "It is the wisdom that comes with age"

Icons
- Writer Ann Landers
- Writer and television personality Martha Stewart
- Child support activist Suzanne Thibodeau
- Talk show host Oprah Winfrey

CONNECTED ENTHUSIASTS

Key Demographics

POPULATION
- Proportion of Canadian population: 6 per cent
- Proportion of Canadians 30 to 49 years of age: 14 per cent
- Total number in Canada: 1.4 million

OTHER DEMOGRAPHICS
- Higher than average proportion in large cities
- Higher than average proportion in Quebec

Fundamental Motivation

- Traditional and New Communities, and Experience-seeking

Key Values
- Family
- Community
- Hedonism
- Immediate Gratification

Words to Live By

- "Age is a state of mind"
- "Live for today"
- "Eat, drink and be merry, for tomorrow we may die"
- "Consistency is the virtue of small minds"
- "Forever young"

Icons

- Playwright Robert Lepage
- Actress Shirley MacLaine
- Pop star Madonna

DISENGAGED DARWINISTS

Key Demographics

POPULATION
- Proportion of Canadian population: 18 per cent
- Proportion of Canadians 30 to 49 years of age: 41 per cent
- Total number in Canada: 4.3 million

OTHER DEMOGRAPHICS
- Higher than average proportion are men
- Higher than average proportion in the Greater Toronto Area
- Higher than average proportion of blue-collar workers

Fundamental Motivation

- Financial Independence, Stability and Security

Key Values
- Fear
- Nostalgia for the Past

Words to Live By

- "It's the law of the jungle"
- "Every man for himself"
- "Look out for Number One"
- "Eat or be eaten"
- "Survival of the fittest"

Icons
- Columnist Barbara Amiel
- Film maker Pierre Falardeau
- Author David Frum
- Actor Chuck Norris

The Gen Xers

THRILL-SEEKING
MATERIALISTS
25%

AIMLESS
DEPENDENTS
27%

SOCIAL
HEDONISTS
15%

NEW
AQUARIANS
13%

AUTONOMOUS
POST-MATERIALISTS
20%

AIMLESS DEPENDENTS

Key Demographics

POPULATION
- Proportion of Canadian population: 8 per cent
- Proportion of Canadians 15 to 29 years of age: 27 per cent
- Total number in Canada: 1.9 million

OTHER DEMOGRAPHICS
- Mostly mirror the general population age 15-29

Fundamental Motivation

- Financial Independence, Stability and Security

Key Values
- Fear
- Desire for Independence

Words to Live By

- "Couldn't care less"
- "It's all meaningless"
- "What's the point?"
- "Damned if you do, damned if you don't"
- "What's the system going to do for me?"

Icons

- Hockey player Eric Lindros
- Singer Courtney Love
- Musical group Smashing Pumpkins

THRILL-SEEKING MATERIALISTS

Key Demographics

POPULATION
- Proportion of Canadian population: 7 per cent
- Proportion of Canadians 15 to 29 years of age: 25 per cent
- Total number in Canada: 1.7 million

OTHER DEMOGRAPHICS
- Higher than average proportion in Toronto

Fundamental Motivation

- Traditional Communities, Social Status and Experience-seeking

Key Values
- Desire for Money and Material Possessions
- Desire for Recognition, Respect and Admiration

Words to Live By
- "Live dangerously"
- "Money is power"
- "It's not how you play the game, it's whether or not you win"
- "Second place is the first loser"

Icons
- Actress Pamela Lee Anderson
- Designer Calvin Klein

NEW AQUARIANS

Key Demographics

POPULATION
- Proportion of Canadian population: 4 per cent
- Proportion of Canadians 15 to 29 years of age: 13 per cent
- Total number in Canada: 900,000

OTHER DEMOGRAPHICS
- Higher than average proportion are teenagers

Fundamental Motivation

- Experience-seeking and New Communities

Key Values
- Egalitarianism
- Ecologism
- Hedonism

Words to Live By
- "There is no being, only becoming"
- "Everything is interconnected"
- "Unity in diversity"

Icons
- Singer Tori Amos
- Author William Gibson
- Software entrepreneur Daniel Langlois
- Singer Sarah McLachlan

AUTONOMOUS POST-MATERIALISTS

Key Demographics

POPULATION
- Proportion of Canadian population: 6 per cent
- Proportion of Canadians 15 to 29 years of age: 20 per cent
- Total number in Canada: 1.4 million

OTHER DEMOGRAPHICS
- Higher than average proportion are in affluent households

Fundamental Motivation
- Personal Autonomy and Self-Fulfilment

Key Values
- Freedom
- Respect for Human Rights

Words to Live By
- "It's My Life"
- "Do your own thing"
- "Image is nothing"
- "There's more to life than money"

Icons
- Musician Ashley MacIsaac
- Publisher Richard Martineau
- Basketball star Dennis Rodman
- Animated character *Bart Simpson* from "The Simpsons"
- Action heroine *Xena, Warrior Princess*

SOCIAL HEDONISTS

Key Demographics

POPULATION
- Proportion of Canadian population: 4 per cent
- Proportion of Canadians 15 to 29 years of age: 15 per cent
- Total number in Canada: 900,000

OTHER DEMOGRAPHICS
- Higher than average proportion in Ontario and Quebec

Fundamental Motivation
- Experience-seeking and New Communities

Key Values
- Aesthetics
- Hedonism
- Sexual Permissiveness
- Immediate Gratification

Words to Live By
- "Don't worry, be happy"
- "There is nothing deeper than the skin"
- "If you look good, you feel good"
- "Party hard"

Icons
- Singer Janet Jackson
- DJ Chris Sheppard
- Race car driver Jacques Villeneuve

Notes

1   George Gallup and Saul Rae, *The Pulse of Democracy* (New York: Simon & Schuster, 1940).

2   Joe Berridge, *The Globe and Mail,* June 22, 1996.

3   Gallup Canada, *The Gallup Poll,* June 17, 1996.

4   Sherry Turkle, *Life on the Screen: Identity in the Age of the Internet* (New York: Simon & Schuster, 1995).

5   Gail Sheehy, *New Passages* (New York: Random House, 1995).

6   Peter Howell, *The Toronto Star*, June 29, 1995.

7   Environics Research Group, *The Media Study* (1995).

8   Statistics Canada, reported in *The Toronto Star,* July 26, 1996.

9   Clifford Stoll, *Silicon Snake Oil* (New York: Doubleday, 1995).

10   Mark Slouka, *War of the Worlds* (New York: BasicBooks, 1995).

11   Marty Rimm, "Marketing Pornography on the Information Superhighway," *Georgetown Law Journal*, Vol. 83, Issue 5.

12   Rosalind Resnick, *1995 Survey of Women Online*
      (New York: Interactive Communications
      Enterprises, 1995).

13   Kate Fillion, *Lip Service* (Toronto: HarperCollins, 1995).

14   Reginald Bibby, quoted in *Western Report,* June
      10, 1996.

15   Ben Wattenberg, *Values Matter Most* (New York:
      The Free Press, 1995).

16   Neil Bissoondath, *Saturday Night*, October, 1994,
      p. 20.

17   Bruce Little, *The Globe and Mail*, July 10, 1995.

18   James Laxer, *The Toronto Star,* July 16, 1995.

19   Graham Fraser, headline of *The Globe and Mail*,
      July 15, 1995.

20   Jean Dumas quoted by Fabrice Taylor, *The Globe
      and Mail,* July 8, 1995.

21   Elaine Carey, *The Toronto Star*, July 31, 1996.

22   *The Toronto Star*, July 11, 1995.

23   Carol Goar, *The Toronto Star*, May 14, 1995.